Dear reader,

Early on in my career as a brain researcher, I had an ....as sure would bring me tons of funding for my work. I decided to use brain imaging devices to investigate the best way to stimulate our brains.

After twenty years of research, I believe I've found the answer. The best way to stimulate the brain is to perform simple mathematical calculations quickly, and to read books aloud. Surprising ? Possibly. But as you will see in the coming pages, these two activities light up the brain like a switchboard.

With some added research, I found that these two activities can even help people retain mental clarity and stave off the mental effects of aging. I used these results to create a brain health workbook called *Train Your Brain*, hoping that I could help make brain health an important social priority.

In 2003, *Train Your Brain* was published in Japan. To everyone's shock, this book became an instant hit, eventually selling millions of copies! As a result of the book, I constantly receive warm messages from people who tell me "your book made exercising my brain part of my daily activity" and "your therapy has improved my memory and made me more energetic." This really delights me because I feel it is a wonderful thing to be able to help others through one's work.

Now, I am very pleased to be able to make a new, updated version of *Train Your Brain* available to people outside of Japan. I believe many readers around the world will find this book extremely beneficial.

It's important to realize that, just as you exercise your body, you must regularly stimulate and exercise your brain. This is the secret to remaining young mentally. So, if you want to stay young at heart, and sharp mentally, take a few minutes a day to *Train Your Brain*!

Sincerely,   Prof. Ryuta Kawashima MD

Table of Contents

Introduction 5-12

Day 1 - Day 5 13-22
Week 1 Prefrontal Cortex Evaluation 23,24
Day 6 - Day 10 25-34
Week 2 Prefrontal Cortex Evaluation 35,36
Day 11 - Day 15.. 37-46
Week 3 Prefrontal Cortex Evaluation 47,48
Day 16 - Day 20.. 49-58
Week 4 Prefrontal Cortex Evaluation 59,60
Day 21 - Day 25.. 61-70
Week 5 Prefrontal Cortex Evaluation 71,72
Day 26 - Day 30.. 73-82
Week 6 Prefrontal Cortex Evaluation 83,84
Day 31 - Day 35.. 85-94
Week 7 Prefrontal Cortex Evaluation 95,96
Day 36 - Day 40.. 97-106
Week 8 Prefrontal Cortex Evaluation 107,108
Day 41 - Day 45.. 109-118
Week 9 Prefrontal Cortex Evaluation 119,120
Day 46 - Day 50.. 121-130
Week 10 Prefrontal Cortex Evaluation................................. 131,132
Day 51 - Day 55.. 133-142
Week 11 Prefrontal Cortex Evaluation................................. 143,144
Day 56 - Day 60.. 145-154
Week 12 Prefrontal Cortex Evaluation................................. 155,156

Answers.. 157-172

Appendix
Pre-training Prefrontal Cortex Evaluation............................ i - iii
Stroop Test .... iv - xv

My Brain Training Chart

Introduction

Ryuta Kawashima
M.D., Tohoku University

Why should you train your brain?

This workbook was created to help you rejuvenate your brain and develop its function to a higher level. Brain function naturally begins to deteriorate after you turn twenty, just like our physical and muscular strength gradually weaken as we age. However, just as you can maintain your physical strength if you exercise regularly, you can keep your brain power from deteriorating by providing daily stimulation for your brain.

In my neuroscience lab, I developed the exercises in this book in order to activate the largest regions of the brain. These brain health exercises increase the delivery of oxygen, blood, and various amino acids to the prefrontal cortex. The result is more neurons and neural connections, which are characteristics of a healthy brain.

Who is this book for?

• **Adults with the following symptoms:**

★ Increasing forgetfulness
★ Difficulty remembering people's names, spelling words, or expressing thoughts.

• **Adults who wish to work on the following:**

★ Creativity
★ Memory skills
★ Communication skills
★ Slowing the mental effects of aging

How can you keep your brain healthy?

In order to maintain your physical health, you have to (1) exercise regularly, (2) eat healthily and (3) sleep well. In like manner, in order to keep your brain healthy, you need to (1) exercise your brain regularly, (2) eat healthily and (3) sleep well. As an adult, you are responsible for your own diet and sleep on a daily basis. This book is exclusively designed to help you get used to also training your brain every day.

Simple calculations really work!

While browsing through this workbook, you may have noticed it consists only of simple calculations. Some of you may be wondering why an adult, who is intellectually active at work and at home, would need to do such elementary school-level math. Through my research I found that simple calculations activate the brain more effectively than any other activity. I also discovered that the best way to activate the largest regions of the brain was to solve these calculations quickly. That is why I have created the easy-to-solve problems you see in this workbook to help you Train Your Brain!

Calculation and oral reading exercises are the optimal training methods according to the latest brain research

My latest research proved that reading aloud, solving simple calculations, and writing activate the brain most effectively.

The pictures on the right show images of the brain taken by a brain-imaging device during various activities (see note 1 on page 12). The red color on the images indicates an increase in regional cerebral blood flow, while the yellow color indicates a larger increase in blood flow to areas where brain activity is most vigorous.

Let's take a look at the images in Charts B and C. Notice that while you are solving calculation problems quickly, there are several red areas in both hemispheres of the brain. Chart B indicates that the visual area at the posterior part of the brain is actively working. Other active parts are the inferior temporal gyrus, which detects the shapes of numbers; Wernicke's area, which recognizes the meanings of words; the angular gyrus, which is the area for calculating; and most importantly, the prefrontal cortex, which is the area for thinking and learning. In comparison, Chart C shows your brain while you are solving simple calculations slowly. The same parts of the brain are working, but the active areas are smaller in size. Solving difficult calculations, surprisingly, does not activate much of your prefrontal cortex at all (see Chart D).

While you are thinking and watching TV, (see charts A and E) most of the different parts of the brain are barely functioning. These charts show that solving simple calculations quickly is the most effective way of activating your brain.

A While you are thinking

left hemisphere   right hemisphere

anterior   posterior   anterior

This is the state of your brain while you are deep in thought. Note the tiny active part in the left hemisphere of the prefrontal cortex (see note 2 on page 12).

E While you are watching TV

left hemisphere   right hemisphere

This is the state of your brain while you are watching TV. The only active parts in either hemisphere of the brain are the visual-oriented occipital lobe and the audio-oriented temporal lobe (See note 2).

B While you are solving simple calculation problems quickly

left hemisphere   right hemisphere

This is the state of your brain while you are quickly solving simple calculations of the kind contained in this book. As you can see, multiple parts of both hemispheres of the brain are actively working. Note how active the prefrontal cortex is.

C While you are solving simple calculations slowly

left hemisphere   right hemisphere

This is the state of your brain while you are slowly solving simple calculations of the kind contained in this book. You can see that the brain is much more active when you solve calculations quickly.

D While you are solving difficult calculations

left hemisphere   right hemisphere

This is the state of your brain while you are solving difficult calculations. A part of the pre-frontal cortex and a part of the left hemisphere of the brain are activated. Note the inactive state of the right hemisphere of the brain.

F While you are writing

left hemisphere   right hemisphere

This is the state of your brain while you are writing. Note the vigorous state of the prefrontal cortex in both hemispheres of the brain.

G While you are silently reading

left hemisphere   right hemisphere

This is the state of your brain while you are silently reading. Many different regions in both hemispheres of the brain are activated.

H While you are reading aloud

left hemisphere   right hemisphere

This is the state of your brain while you are reading aloud. Active areas in both hemi-spheres of the brain are much larger than in Chart G. Research has also shown that the brain becomes more active when you read faster.

Brain training boosted the ability to remember by twenty percent

My research team carried out research with elementary school students. We counted how many words they could memorize within two minutes and found that, on average, they could memorize 8.3 words. When we conducted the same test after a two-minute calculation exercise, the average word count remembered increased to 9.8. Our results show that these exercises boosted the children's ability to remember by more than twenty percent.

The calculation exercises acted as a warm-up for the students, allowing them to perform better on the word memorization tests.

Simple calculation and oral reading exercises alleviated symptoms of dementia

My team also conducted an experiment with twelve dementia Alzheimer type patients. We gave our patients a ten-minutes-a-day writing and oral reading exercise and a ten-minutes-a-day calculation exercise to be performed two to five days a week. Cognitive and prefrontal cortex function of non-participant subjects that did not do the calculation and oral reading exercises deteriorated during the six-month follow up. However, with participant subjects that did do the exercises, we succeeded in preventing deterioration of their cognitive function, as well as improving their prefrontal cortex function.

This is an exceptional achievement on a global scale - rarely has the deterioration of the cognitive function of dementia Alzheimer type patients been slowed or diminished.

1 Change in word memorization

Word count

Before training — After training

2 Change in cognitive function

MMS scores [*1]

Participant subjects with mild symptoms of dementia

Non-participant subjects with mild symptoms of dementia

Participant subjects with heavy symptoms of dementia

Non-participant subjects with heavy symptoms of dementia

Before training   Three months later   Six months late

* 1 MMS.tests evaluate your cognitive abilities such as comprehension and judgme

3 Change in prefrontal cortex function

FAB score [*2]

Non-participant subjects with mild symptoms of dementia

Participant subjects with mild symptoms of dementia

Non-participant subjects with heavy symptoms of dementia

Participant subjects with heavy symptoms of dementia

Before training   Three months later   Six months late

* 2 FAB tests evaluate your prefrontal cortex function by testing your abilities to communicate and control behavior.

How to train your brain using this book

1 First, check how well your brain is functioning currently

Check the status of your brain function by using the Pre-training Prefrontal Cortex Evaluation. Please see instruction **5** to learn more about evaluation procedures.

2 Train your brain a few minutes every day

The most crucial point in any kind of training is continuity. It is ideal to train your brain in the morning, when your brain is the most active. It is also important to eat before you do the calculation exercise; otherwise, the effects will be reduced by half.

Many of you may have noticed it takes you more time to calculate in the afternoon and at night than in the morning. That is because the brain functions more effectively in the morning than at any other time of the day. I suggest you carry out the exercises at the same hour every day, if possible.

3 Tips for the program

Please solve the calculation problems on the front and back of one worksheet each day. Try to solve the problems quickly, but do not worry if you make mistakes or are slow at first. All evaluations are only for the purposes of tracking your own progress.

Worksheet target time

- **One minute :**
Gold Medal. If you often calculate manually, or regularly use math at work, you may be able to achieve this target. In other words, you can call yourself a Numbers Whiz if you reach this level.

- **One and a half minutes :**
Silver Medal. With continued effort, you can reach this level. If you do achieve this goal, your calculation abilities must be higher than average. You may call yourself a Calculation Expert.

- **Two minutes :**
Bronze Medal. You will be able to attain this level if you set your mind to it - please keep working toward this goal. If you do attain this level, you should be known as a Calculation Master.

4 Stop and evaluate after every fifth day

This 60-Day Calculation Exercise Program is comprised of calculation worksheets to be solved one per day from Monday through Friday and Prefrontal Cortex Evaluations to be taken during weekends. If you do not wish to stop training during weekends, or if your busy schedule does not allow you to study every weekday as I recommend, then take the Prefrontal Cortex Evaluation after every five study days.

After completing each Evaluation, please record your results in My Brain Training Chart at the end of the appendix. You may clearly recognize positive changes in your brain as you log the results each week (see note 3 on page 12). Please try to exercise continuously; if there is an interval between exercises, the effects may become less noticeable.

Counting Test

Measure the time required for you to count the numbers from 1 to 120 aloud as fast as you can. You must pronounce every number articulately. This test evaluates the general function of the prefrontal cortex in both the left and right hemispheres. Research has shown that the results of counting tests like this one are closely related to the mathematical abilities of each person. Please set your own goal and try to achieve your personal target time.

5 How to evaluate your prefrontal cortex

Before starting your calculation program, please take the Pre-Training Prefrontal Cortex Evaluation. After you start your training, please evaluate your prefrontal cortex after every five study days using the Prefrontal Cortex Evaluations at the end of the book. It may be a good idea to have a member of your family or a friend measure the time required for you to solve the problems.

Word Memorization Test

Each word list consists of 30 simple words. Please memorize as many words as you can within two minutes. After two minutes, turn the paper over and write down as many words as you can remember. The number of correct answers will be your score. The aim of this test is to evaluate your prefrontal cortex activity in the left hemisphere, which is linked to short-term memory.

Please get used to the procedure by first using the chart at the top of each Stroop Test. Then proceed to the test. Measure and record the time required for you to name all of the colors. The aim of this test is to evaluate the general function of your prefrontal cortex area in both the left and right hemispheres. There are no target times or scores, as the results of the test vary greatly according to individuals. Please just try to do better than your previous week's results.

■ Example

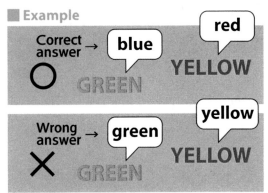

* If you make a mistake, please go back to where you made the mistake and start over.

Stroop Test

At the end of the book, you will see a chart of color names. Often the color names are printed in a color different from the color they actually label. The test requires you to *say the color the word is printed in aloud*. In other words, if you see the word "Blue" printed in red ink, you should say "Red," not "Blue." Try to ignore the words that you see, and report only the color of the ink.

6 When you're finished with this workbook...

Now that calculation has become a part of your daily routine, it is important to continue your calculation exercise every day. Once you stop training your brain, your brain function will begin to decline again slowly. Please go back to Day 1 of the book and repeat the training.

• Note 1 :

Brain-imaging devices create three-dimensional images of human brain function without harming the body or the brain. Functional magnetic resonance imaging (fMRI) and near-infrared spectroscopy are the two major technologies used in brain science studies at this time.

fMRI apparatus

• Note 2 :

There are four parts in both hemispheres of the human brain which control individual function: the frontal lobe (motor function), the parietal lobe (tactile sense), the temporal lobe (auditory perception), and the occipital lobe (visual sense).

The prefrontal region, which makes up a large part of the frontal lobe, is the distinctive feature of the human brain and is the foundation of creativity, memory, communication, and self-control.

The brain as seen from the left side

angular gyrus
prefrontal cortex
Wernicke's area
visual cortex
parietal lobe
frontal lobe
occipital lobe
temporal lobe
anterior   inferior
temporal gyrus
posterior

• Note 3 :

At the onset of this training your brain function will improve somewhat steadily. However, you will probably hit a wall at a certain point. You may wonder why your results are not showing any sign of improvement. But if you hang in there and continue your training, a breakthrough will come, and you will see your scores suddenly jump. If you are facing doldrums, just remember that your brain is preparing for a leap.

Your brain power

Time spent for training

Day 1

Before you start, please take the Pre-training Prefrontal Cortex Evaluation.

Date ___ M ___ D

Start Time ___ : ___

$4 + 5 =$ ___

$2 \times 4 =$ ___

$8 - 3 =$ ___

$3 + 8 =$ ___

$12 - 6 =$ ___

$9 \times 7 =$ ___

$5 - 4 =$ ___

$6 \times 4 =$ ___

$1 + 6 =$ ___

$11 - 7 =$ ___

$3 \times 0 =$ ___

$9 + 1 =$ ___

$6 \times 6 =$ ___

$9 \times 5 =$ ___

$14 - 5 =$ ___

$8 + 3 =$ ___

$1 \times 5 =$ ___

$7 + 6 =$ ___

$14 - 8 =$ ___

$1 + 5 =$ ___

$2 \times 8 =$ ___

$16 - 7 =$ ___

$5 + 6 =$ ___

$3 - 3 =$ ___

$9 + 9 =$ ___

$2 \times 3 =$ ___

$8 - 5 =$ ___

$5 \times 8 =$ ___

$15 - 7 =$ ___

$2 + 9 =$ ___

$8 \times 9 =$ ___

$2 + 5 =$ ___

$9 - 6 =$ ___

$7 - 7 =$ ___

$3 + 2 =$ ___

$3 \times 6 =$ ___

$9 \times 2 =$ ___

$4 + 7 =$ ___

$10 - 6 =$ ___

$9 \times 8 =$ ___

$6 + 0 =$ ___

$1 + 9 =$ ___

$14 - 9 =$ ___

$11 - 4 =$ ___

$2 \times 9 =$ ___

$4 - 2 =$ ___

$2 + 7 =$ ___

$4 \times 6 =$ ___

$13 - 7 =$ ___

$8 + 6 =$ ___

$9 - 3 =$ ☐

$9 + 4 =$ ☐

$2 \times 3 =$ ☐

$11 - 2 =$ ☐

$8 \times 7 =$ ☐

$13 - 7 =$ ☐

$5 + 4 =$ ☐

$12 - 3 =$ ☐

$5 - 2 =$ ☐

$6 \times 0 =$ ☐

$6 + 5 =$ ☐

$16 - 8 =$ ☐

$5 \times 3 =$ ☐

$7 + 0 =$ ☐

$6 + 4 =$ ☐

$11 - 5 =$ ☐

$3 \times 9 =$ ☐

$3 \times 8 =$ ☐

$7 - 3 =$ ☐

$3 + 4 =$ ☐

$5 \times 3 =$ ☐

$7 + 8 =$ ☐

$2 + 2 =$ ☐

$11 - 9 =$ ☐

$4 \times 5 =$ ☐

$2 \times 8 =$ ☐

$9 + 3 =$ ☐

$7 - 5 =$ ☐

$14 - 7 =$ ☐

$9 \times 7 =$ ☐

$7 + 1 =$ ☐

$11 - 3 =$ ☐

$7 \times 5 =$ ☐

$4 + 9 =$ ☐

$3 + 7 =$ ☐

$4 \times 3 =$ ☐

$6 + 7 =$ ☐

$9 - 8 =$ ☐

$10 - 6 =$ ☐

$5 \times 5 =$ ☐

$12 - 3 =$ ☐

$6 + 8 =$ ☐

$6 \times 3 =$ ☐

$4 + 8 =$ ☐

$3 - 1 =$ ☐

$4 + 2 =$ ☐

$9 + 6 =$ ☐

$8 \times 2 =$ ☐

$6 \times 8 =$ ☐

$13 - 5 =$ ☐

End Time ☐ : ☐

Start Time ☐ : ☐

3 × 9 = ☐　　7 + 6 = ☐　　4 × 9 = ☐

11 − 7 = ☐　　13 − 7 = ☐　　5 + 4 = ☐

4 + 3 = ☐　　6 × 7 = ☐　　16 − 8 = ☐

6 + 8 = ☐　　9 + 4 = ☐　　9 + 4 = ☐

3 × 6 = ☐　　11 − 6 = ☐　　4 × 2 = ☐

5 × 4 = ☐　　8 × 0 = ☐　　8 − 5 = ☐

8 + 9 = ☐　　6 × 8 = ☐　　9 + 2 = ☐

8 − 1 = ☐　　1 + 8 = ☐　　6 − 6 = ☐

15 − 6 = ☐　　12 − 3 = ☐　　8 × 6 = ☐

1 × 5 = ☐　　9 − 4 = ☐　　4 × 6 = ☐

0 + 9 = ☐　　8 + 7 = ☐　　12 − 7 = ☐

3 × 3 = ☐　　9 × 5 = ☐　　2 + 4 = ☐

6 − 5 = ☐　　10 − 8 = ☐　　9 − 7 = ☐

5 + 8 = ☐　　7 − 4 = ☐　　7 + 8 = ☐

1 + 2 = ☐　　6 + 1 = ☐　　6 × 2 = ☐

12 − 5 = ☐　　7 × 5 = ☐　　10 − 4 = ☐

　　　　　　1 + 9 = ☐　　7 × 8 = ☐

9 + 3 = ☐

8 × 2 = ☐

10 − 3 = ☐

2 + 5 = ☐

8 − 7 = ☐

9 + 8 = ☐

3 × 5 = ☐

3 + 6 = ☐

4 − 1 = ☐

14 − 6 = ☐

9 × 9 = ☐

7 − 5 = ☐

4 + 0 = ☐

10 − 7 = ☐

8 + 5 = ☐

9 + 5 = ☐

3 × 7 = ☐

2 × 3 = ☐

11 − 4 = ☐

4 + 6 = ☐

8 × 5 = ☐

15 − 9 = ☐

2 × 7 = ☐

5 + 9 = ☐

7 + 1 = ☐

10 − 1 = ☐

3 + 4 = ☐

4 × 8 = ☐

8 + 6 = ☐

6 − 2 = ☐

5 × 2 = ☐

9 − 3 = ☐

2 × 6 = ☐

10 − 4 = ☐

8 − 0 = ☐

3 + 9 = ☐

11 − 3 = ☐

7 × 3 = ☐

2 × 4 = ☐

2 + 8 = ☐

7 × 6 = ☐

12 − 4 = ☐

5 + 3 = ☐

6 × 7 = ☐

7 + 3 = ☐

16 − 9 = ☐

9 × 9 = ☐

17 − 8 = ☐

8 × 9 = ☐

9 + 6 = ☐

End Time ☐ : ☐

Start Time ☐ : ☐

13 − 6 =	4 + 6 =	7 × 5 =
7 + 4 =	8 − 8 =	11 − 2 =
14 − 6 =	3 × 1 =	2 × 9 =
3 × 4 =	15 − 8 =	6 + 6 =
10 − 2 =	3 + 1 =	5 − 3 =
4 + 3 =	4 × 7 =	3 × 3 =
5 × 7 =	9 − 6 =	7 + 6 =
8 + 5 =	9 + 3 =	12 − 6 =
8 − 4 =	6 × 4 =	2 × 7 =
1 + 0 =	5 + 9 =	3 + 2 =
8 × 6 =	6 + 2 =	5 + 8 =
13 − 5 =	8 × 6 =	9 × 7 =
2 + 6 =	2 + 3 =	10 − 1 =
4 × 5 =	3 × 7 =	3 − 1 =
4 − 3 =	11 − 3 =	9 + 6 =
8 + 7 =	2 + 8 =	2 × 5 =
	16 − 8 =	9 − 8 =

$8 \times 2 =$ ☐

$12 - 5 =$ ☐

$3 + 2 =$ ☐

$13 - 7 =$ ☐

$3 \times 9 =$ ☐

$5 + 7 =$ ☐

$9 - 9 =$ ☐

$3 \times 6 =$ ☐

$7 \times 3 =$ ☐

$16 - 7 =$ ☐

$7 + 1 =$ ☐

$6 + 5 =$ ☐

$8 - 0 =$ ☐

$9 + 9 =$ ☐

$12 - 7 =$ ☐

$8 \times 4 =$ ☐

$8 - 7 =$ ☐

$6 - 3 =$ ☐

$4 + 8 =$ ☐

$9 \times 6 =$ ☐

$5 + 3 =$ ☐

$1 \times 6 =$ ☐

$2 + 9 =$ ☐

$5 \times 0 =$ ☐

$15 - 7 =$ ☐

$9 + 4 =$ ☐

$4 \times 6 =$ ☐

$7 \times 2 =$ ☐

$3 \times 8 =$ ☐

$7 + 3 =$ ☐

$6 - 4 =$ ☐

$2 \times 3 =$ ☐

$14 - 8 =$ ☐

$4 + 4 =$ ☐

$11 - 5 =$ ☐

$6 \times 8 =$ ☐

$8 + 3 =$ ☐

$3 + 6 =$ ☐

$15 - 6 =$ ☐

$6 + 4 =$ ☐

$4 \times 9 =$ ☐

$5 - 2 =$ ☐

$9 + 5 =$ ☐

$6 \times 2 =$ ☐

$17 - 8 =$ ☐

$8 + 0 =$ ☐

$6 \times 6 =$ ☐

$7 + 7 =$ ☐

$11 - 8 =$ ☐

$7 \times 8 =$ ☐

End Time [ ] : [ ]

Start Time ☐ : ☐

9 + 5 = ☐

10 − 5 = ☐

3 × 6 = ☐

4 + 9 = ☐

5 × 4 = ☐

9 − 6 = ☐

0 + 8 = ☐

2 × 2 = ☐

12 − 5 = ☐

8 + 6 = ☐

7 × 7 = ☐

3 × 1 = ☐

1 + 5 = ☐

7 − 4 = ☐

8 + 9 = ☐

2 × 7 = ☐

8 × 9 = ☐

11 − 6 = ☐

2 + 4 = ☐

7 − 6 = ☐

9 × 4 = ☐

14 − 6 = ☐

4 + 6 = ☐

5 − 1 = ☐

4 + 8 = ☐

7 × 4 = ☐

12 − 9 = ☐

2 × 5 = ☐

8 − 6 = ☐

8 + 8 = ☐

4 × 2 = ☐

10 − 4 = ☐

4 + 5 = ☐

7 + 5 = ☐

2 + 7 = ☐

8 × 4 = ☐

13 − 5 = ☐

3 + 7 = ☐

9 − 8 = ☐

9 × 2 = ☐

14 − 7 = ☐

8 + 1 = ☐

12 − 4 = ☐

5 × 5 = ☐

3 + 4 = ☐

9 − 4 = ☐

15 − 7 = ☐

6 × 8 = ☐

3 × 7 = ☐

8 + 5 = ☐

6 − 2 = ☐

4 × 6 = ☐

7 + 3 = ☐

9 × 3 = ☐

15 − 8 = ☐

4 + 4 = ☐

3 × 1 = ☐

9 + 4 = ☐

14 − 5 = ☐

4 × 4 = ☐

11 − 3 = ☐

0 + 6 = ☐

9 + 9 = ☐

5 × 1 = ☐

7 × 9 = ☐

14 − 7 = ☐

5 + 9 = ☐

7 + 4 = ☐

2 × 8 = ☐

12 − 6 = ☐

1 + 8 = ☐

10 − 6 = ☐

5 + 6 = ☐

9 × 6 = ☐

7 − 3 = ☐

8 + 4 = ☐

5 × 2 = ☐

8 − 1 = ☐

4 × 7 = ☐

2 + 5 = ☐

15 − 6 = ☐

2 + 8 = ☐

3 × 6 = ☐

8 − 5 = ☐

11 − 5 = ☐

7 × 8 = ☐

4 − 2 = ☐

7 + 6 = ☐

9 × 5 = ☐

10 − 8 = ☐

2 × 6 = ☐

3 + 8 = ☐

16 − 9 = ☐

9 − 8 = ☐

5 × 6 = ☐

8 + 0 = ☐

9 + 7 = ☐

7 × 6 = ☐

6 + 3 = ☐

13 − 6 = ☐

End Time ☐ : ☐

Date ⬚ M ⬚ D

Start Time ⬚ : ⬚

7 − 2 = ⬚

1 + 3 = ⬚

6 × 9 = ⬚

3 × 1 = ⬚

5 + 9 = ⬚

2 × 6 = ⬚

16 − 8 = ⬚

9 + 6 = ⬚

5 − 5 = ⬚

7 × 9 = ⬚

14 − 5 = ⬚

7 − 1 = ⬚

2 × 4 = ⬚

3 + 8 = ⬚

9 × 3 = ⬚

9 + 1 = ⬚

13 − 6 = ⬚

5 × 7 = ⬚

3 + 9 = ⬚

7 × 6 = ⬚

8 − 2 = ⬚

4 + 0 = ⬚

7 + 9 = ⬚

3 × 6 = ⬚

15 − 8 = ⬚

3 + 3 = ⬚

7 + 6 = ⬚

12 − 5 = ⬚

8 × 7 = ⬚

9 − 0 = ⬚

3 × 8 = ⬚

4 × 4 = ⬚

4 + 8 = ⬚

4 + 7 = ⬚

3 + 5 = ⬚

4 × 8 = ⬚

12 − 6 = ⬚

2 + 8 = ⬚

7 − 3 = ⬚

5 + 4 = ⬚

0 × 0 = ⬚

13 − 8 = ⬚

5 × 3 = ⬚

3 + 6 = ⬚

10 − 4 = ⬚

9 − 9 = ⬚

8 + 9 = ⬚

15 − 6 = ⬚

2 × 8 = ⬚

2 + 4 = ⬚

$4 \times 6 =$ [　]　　$2 + 5 =$ [　]　　$11 - 9 =$ [　]

$2 + 9 =$ [　]　　$17 - 9 =$ [　]　　$7 + 7 =$ [　]

$11 - 3 =$ [　]　　$7 \times 4 =$ [　]　　$3 \times 2 =$ [　]

$9 \times 8 =$ [　]　　$8 + 2 =$ [　]　　$14 - 6 =$ [　]

$2 - 2 =$ [　]　　$2 \times 8 =$ [　]　　$7 \times 8 =$ [　]

$6 + 7 =$ [　]　　$13 - 7 =$ [　]　　$6 + 9 =$ [　]

$13 - 5 =$ [　]　　$8 \times 1 =$ [　]　　$7 - 5 =$ [　]

$3 + 9 =$ [　]　　$4 + 4 =$ [　]　　$4 + 3 =$ [　]

$4 \times 3 =$ [　]　　$9 \times 6 =$ [　]　　$10 - 8 =$ [　]

$5 - 4 =$ [　]　　$8 + 3 =$ [　]　　$9 \times 5 =$ [　]

$8 \times 9 =$ [　]　　$5 \times 2 =$ [　]　　$2 + 6 =$ [　]

$8 - 5 =$ [　]　　$10 - 5 =$ [　]　　$16 - 9 =$ [　]

$7 + 8 =$ [　]　　$2 + 7 =$ [　]　　$5 - 4 =$ [　]

$1 + 6 =$ [　]　　$4 \times 7 =$ [　]　　$6 \times 7 =$ [　]

$13 - 9 =$ [　]　　$12 - 4 =$ [　]　　$9 + 4 =$ [　]

$3 \times 6 =$ [　]　　$6 + 8 =$ [　]　　$18 - 9 =$ [　]

$5 \times 5 =$ [　]　　$8 - 3 =$ [　]

End Time [ ] : [ ]

I. Counting Test

Measure the time required for you to count from 1 to 120 aloud as fast as you can.

☐ sec.

II. Word Memorization Test

Memorize as many words as you can **within two minutes.**

sand	hope	degree	farm	tennis	age
iron	mountain	sight	room	plain	engine
blood	chance	dream	subject	laugh	pattern
crystal	figure	week	noise	space	ring
tea	voice	goat	map	carrot	shoe

Write out as many words as you can remember **in two minutes** on the back of this page. How many words can you remember?

Number of words memorized ☐ words

Word Memorization Test Answers

III. Stroop Test

Please take the **Stroop Test** for Week 1, located on page **iv** of the Appendix.

Start Time ☐ : ☐

8 + 2 =

11 − 4 =

2 + 5 =

6 × 4 =

18 − 9 =

7 + 5 =

7 − 7 =

5 + 8 =

9 × 7 =

6 − 4 =

7 × 2 =

10 − 5 =

6 + 5 =

2 × 9 =

8 + 0 =

5 − 3 =

7 − 2 =

3 + 3 =

4 × 3 =

9 × 3 =

8 + 4 =

16 − 7 =

3 × 2 =

7 + 1 =

9 + 9 =

6 × 6 =

14 − 6 =

7 × 8 =

9 − 5 =

4 + 5 =

6 × 7 =

11 − 2 =

9 + 1 =

4 × 8 =

1 + 5 =

5 × 3 =

5 − 0 =

6 + 8 =

12 − 7 =

4 × 1 =

8 − 3 =

3 × 7 =

6 + 1 =

10 − 9 =

6 × 2 =

5 + 7 =

5 × 9 =

7 × 7 =

12 − 9 =

9 + 3 =

$2 \times 7 =$ ☐ $9 + 8 =$ ☐ $6 - 5 =$ ☐

$5 - 1 =$ ☐ $4 \times 2 =$ ☐ $5 + 5 =$ ☐

$1 + 4 =$ ☐ $5 + 7 =$ ☐ $3 \times 8 =$ ☐

$9 \times 9 =$ ☐ $9 - 3 =$ ☐ $14 - 9 =$ ☐

$2 + 8 =$ ☐ $14 - 5 =$ ☐ $8 \times 2 =$ ☐

$3 + 4 =$ ☐ $7 \times 6 =$ ☐ $13 - 4 =$ ☐

$11 - 8 =$ ☐ $12 - 3 =$ ☐ $3 + 6 =$ ☐

$2 \times 1 =$ ☐ $1 + 9 =$ ☐ $10 - 1 =$ ☐

$5 \times 4 =$ ☐ $6 \times 3 =$ ☐ $8 - 6 =$ ☐

$7 + 6 =$ ☐ $4 + 8 =$ ☐ $6 \times 5 =$ ☐

$6 - 6 =$ ☐ $7 - 0 =$ ☐ $3 + 9 =$ ☐

$17 - 8 =$ ☐ $4 + 2 =$ ☐ $14 - 7 =$ ☐

$3 \times 9 =$ ☐ $7 + 7 =$ ☐ $6 \times 8 =$ ☐

$2 + 2 =$ ☐ $4 \times 6 =$ ☐ $5 + 4 =$ ☐

$15 - 8 =$ ☐ $2 \times 5 =$ ☐ $4 + 9 =$ ☐

$4 \times 4 =$ ☐ $11 - 9 =$ ☐ $13 - 6 =$ ☐

$8 + 6 =$ ☐ $5 \times 5 =$ ☐

End Time ☐ : ☐

Start Time ☐ : ☐

14 − 9 = ☐

5 × 8 = ☐

9 + 3 = ☐

11 − 2 = ☐

6 × 2 = ☐

0 × 7 = ☐

2 + 6 = ☐

12 − 4 = ☐

7 − 2 = ☐

4 + 8 = ☐

2 × 1 = ☐

10 − 2 = ☐

4 − 1 = ☐

3 + 2 = ☐

8 × 3 = ☐

7 + 3 = ☐

5 × 2 = ☐

6 + 1 = ☐

11 − 6 = ☐

1 + 9 = ☐

9 × 3 = ☐

8 − 7 = ☐

6 + 5 = ☐

9 − 4 = ☐

2 × 9 = ☐

5 × 7 = ☐

12 − 7 = ☐

2 + 4 = ☐

7 − 4 = ☐

3 + 9 = ☐

7 × 6 = ☐

15 − 8 = ☐

4 × 6 = ☐

5 + 7 = ☐

9 × 8 = ☐

17 − 9 = ☐

5 + 2 = ☐

8 + 2 = ☐

5 × 5 = ☐

2 × 8 = ☐

8 + 5 = ☐

9 − 8 = ☐

13 − 7 = ☐

6 × 5 = ☐

1 + 5 = ☐

3 × 2 = ☐

6 − 4 = ☐

9 + 8 = ☐

4 + 5 = ☐

12 − 9 = ☐

$3 \times 5 =$ [ ]

$11 - 7 =$ [ ]

$4 + 6 =$ [ ]

$4 \times 3 =$ [ ]

$13 - 5 =$ [ ]

$2 \times 4 =$ [ ]

$6 + 9 =$ [ ]

$1 + 7 =$ [ ]

$10 - 9 =$ [ ]

$7 + 4 =$ [ ]

$6 \times 2 =$ [ ]

$8 + 7 =$ [ ]

$7 - 2 =$ [ ]

$2 \times 5 =$ [ ]

$3 - 2 =$ [ ]

$4 \times 9 =$ [ ]

$14 - 6 =$ [ ]

$6 - 3 =$ [ ]

$9 + 2 =$ [ ]

$13 - 5 =$ [ ]

$6 \times 4 =$ [ ]

$9 \times 1 =$ [ ]

$6 + 5 =$ [ ]

$8 \times 6 =$ [ ]

$13 - 9 =$ [ ]

$8 + 1 =$ [ ]

$9 \times 2 =$ [ ]

$7 + 6 =$ [ ]

$16 - 8 =$ [ ]

$7 \times 3 =$ [ ]

$18 - 9 =$ [ ]

$4 \times 8 =$ [ ]

$7 + 7 =$ [ ]

$4 \times 7 =$ [ ]

$9 + 7 =$ [ ]

$3 \times 0 =$ [ ]

$5 - 5 =$ [ ]

$7 + 0 =$ [ ]

$16 - 7 =$ [ ]

$5 + 8 =$ [ ]

$9 \times 5 =$ [ ]

$6 + 2 =$ [ ]

$9 - 5 =$ [ ]

$10 - 8 =$ [ ]

$8 \times 7 =$ [ ]

$8 - 4 =$ [ ]

$7 + 2 =$ [ ]

$9 + 1 =$ [ ]

$10 - 8 =$ [ ]

$7 + 9 =$ [ ]

End Time [ ] : [ ]

Date ☐ M ☐ D

Start Time ☐ : ☐

7 − 4 = ☐

3 × 5 = ☐

12 − 8 = ☐

7 + 2 = ☐

4 × 3 = ☐

1 − 1 = ☐

9 + 4 = ☐

3 × 2 = ☐

14 − 6 = ☐

3 + 3 = ☐

2 × 4 = ☐

2 + 6 = ☐

2 × 7 = ☐

14 − 8 = ☐

9 + 1 = ☐

10 − 7 = ☐

2 × 5 = ☐

15 − 6 = ☐

6 × 4 = ☐

4 + 9 = ☐

8 − 2 = ☐

4 × 9 = ☐

6 + 4 = ☐

11 − 7 = ☐

6 × 3 = ☐

3 + 5 = ☐

8 + 7 = ☐

1 × 6 = ☐

10 − 2 = ☐

4 − 3 = ☐

7 + 4 = ☐

6 × 6 = ☐

8 − 6 = ☐

8 + 9 = ☐

12 − 3 = ☐

7 + 5 = ☐

4 × 8 = ☐

8 × 6 = ☐

13 − 4 = ☐

1 + 8 = ☐

8 × 9 = ☐

6 + 6 = ☐

9 − 7 = ☐

8 × 5 = ☐

9 × 2 = ☐

11 − 6 = ☐

4 + 3 = ☐

3 × 7 = ☐

5 − 3 = ☐

2 + 8 = ☐

$9 - 5 =$ ☐ $13 - 9 =$ ☐ $7 \times 2 =$ ☐

$3 + 7 =$ ☐ $2 \times 0 =$ ☐ $15 - 8 =$ ☐

$1 \times 6 =$ ☐ $6 + 5 =$ ☐ $1 + 6 =$ ☐

$4 + 2 =$ ☐ $3 + 6 =$ ☐ $6 \times 2 =$ ☐

$5 \times 9 =$ ☐ $14 - 5 =$ ☐ $5 \times 8 =$ ☐

$8 + 4 =$ ☐ $4 + 7 =$ ☐ $7 + 9 =$ ☐

$9 \times 7 =$ ☐ $7 \times 5 =$ ☐ $7 - 6 =$ ☐

$14 - 6 =$ ☐ $3 - 3 =$ ☐ $4 \times 2 =$ ☐

$1 + 9 =$ ☐ $5 + 5 =$ ☐ $6 \times 8 =$ ☐

$8 \times 7 =$ ☐ $3 \times 3 =$ ☐ $15 - 9 =$ ☐

$2 \times 3 =$ ☐ $10 - 3 =$ ☐ $2 + 5 =$ ☐

$10 - 7 =$ ☐ $3 + 1 =$ ☐ $6 + 9 =$ ☐

$3 + 9 =$ ☐ $3 \times 9 =$ ☐ $9 - 3 =$ ☐

$3 - 2 =$ ☐ $5 + 7 =$ ☐ $7 + 8 =$ ☐

$6 \times 5 =$ ☐ $12 - 6 =$ ☐ $16 - 7 =$ ☐

$12 - 9 =$ ☐ $5 \times 6 =$ ☐ $7 \times 8 =$ ☐

$2 + 1 =$ ☐ $8 - 7 =$ ☐

End Time ☐ : ☐

Start Time ☐ : ☐

10 − 2 = ☐

9 + 6 = ☐

4 − 1 = ☐

5 × 6 = ☐

12 − 3 = ☐

1 + 8 = ☐

7 − 2 = ☐

6 + 9 = ☐

8 × 3 = ☐

11 − 4 = ☐

4 × 5 = ☐

6 − 5 = ☐

6 + 6 = ☐

4 × 8 = ☐

13 − 8 = ☐

7 + 2 = ☐

8 + 7 = ☐

5 + 0 = ☐

9 × 4 = ☐

12 − 9 = ☐

4 + 7 = ☐

9 − 0 = ☐

4 × 7 = ☐

15 − 9 = ☐

6 + 3 = ☐

12 − 5 = ☐

1 × 8 = ☐

1 + 2 = ☐

9 − 5 = ☐

15 − 7 = ☐

7 × 4 = ☐

4 × 0 = ☐

9 + 7 = ☐

5 × 3 = ☐

2 + 8 = ☐

11 − 3 = ☐

4 × 2 = ☐

1 + 9 = ☐

9 × 3 = ☐

5 − 4 = ☐

5 + 2 = ☐

8 × 2 = ☐

10 − 8 = ☐

8 + 5 = ☐

4 × 6 = ☐

5 × 9 = ☐

1 + 5 = ☐

8 − 3 = ☐

9 + 8 = ☐

3 × 7 = ☐

$2 + 9 =$ ☐ $16 - 7 =$ ☐ $7 - 3 =$ ☐

$5 \times 1 =$ ☐ $8 \times 6 =$ ☐ $2 \times 9 =$ ☐

$18 - 9 =$ ☐ $8 - 8 =$ ☐ $7 + 6 =$ ☐

$6 + 0 =$ ☐ $5 + 6 =$ ☐ $3 \times 2 =$ ☐

$10 - 9 =$ ☐ $8 \times 4 =$ ☐ $16 - 8 =$ ☐

$7 + 6 =$ ☐ $12 - 7 =$ ☐ $3 + 5 =$ ☐

$7 \times 3 =$ ☐ $7 \times 7 =$ ☐ $7 \times 9 =$ ☐

$7 - 4 =$ ☐ $9 + 9 =$ ☐ $8 + 4 =$ ☐

$3 + 7 =$ ☐ $15 - 8 =$ ☐ $17 - 9 =$ ☐

$5 \times 5 =$ ☐ $3 - 1 =$ ☐ $8 \times 7 =$ ☐

$9 - 3 =$ ☐ $2 \times 2 =$ ☐ $13 - 5 =$ ☐

$3 \times 8 =$ ☐ $4 + 3 =$ ☐ $8 + 1 =$ ☐

$5 + 4 =$ ☐ $9 + 2 =$ ☐ $7 + 9 =$ ☐

$10 - 3 =$ ☐ $4 \times 9 =$ ☐ $9 \times 6 =$ ☐

$9 + 5 =$ ☐ $9 + 0 =$ ☐ $5 \times 7 =$ ☐

$6 \times 4 =$ ☐ $11 - 8 =$ ☐ $14 - 9 =$ ☐

$3 - 3 =$ ☐ $7 + 7 =$ ☐

End Time ☐ : ☐

Date ☐ M ☐ D

Start Time ☐ : ☐

$9 \times 2 =$ ☐

$2 + 8 =$ ☐

$5 \times 7 =$ ☐

$9 - 2 =$ ☐

$3 + 0 =$ ☐

$5 + 7 =$ ☐

$4 \times 1 =$ ☐

$12 - 6 =$ ☐

$8 + 1 =$ ☐

$9 + 4 =$ ☐

$13 - 6 =$ ☐

$3 \times 7 =$ ☐

$7 - 1 =$ ☐

$5 \times 6 =$ ☐

$2 \times 6 =$ ☐

$9 + 6 =$ ☐

$8 + 5 =$ ☐

$2 + 6 =$ ☐

$9 \times 5 =$ ☐

$10 - 9 =$ ☐

$9 + 3 =$ ☐

$7 - 2 =$ ☐

$7 + 1 =$ ☐

$2 \times 6 =$ ☐

$16 - 9 =$ ☐

$4 \times 8 =$ ☐

$8 + 7 =$ ☐

$5 \times 4 =$ ☐

$9 - 8 =$ ☐

$7 + 3 =$ ☐

$10 - 5 =$ ☐

$6 \times 9 =$ ☐

$4 + 4 =$ ☐

$13 - 8 =$ ☐

$3 + 4 =$ ☐

$3 \times 9 =$ ☐

$7 \times 0 =$ ☐

$8 \times 6 =$ ☐

$1 + 9 =$ ☐

$5 \times 9 =$ ☐

$10 - 3 =$ ☐

$7 + 8 =$ ☐

$7 - 3 =$ ☐

$6 \times 3 =$ ☐

$17 - 9 =$ ☐

$3 - 1 =$ ☐

$7 \times 6 =$ ☐

$9 + 2 =$ ☐

$8 \times 4 =$ ☐

$11 - 8 =$ ☐

$8 + 1 =$ ☐ $11 - 2 =$ ☐ $3 \times 5 =$ ☐

$13 - 7 =$ ☐ $3 + 8 =$ ☐ $7 + 5 =$ ☐

$5 \times 2 =$ ☐ $6 \times 9 =$ ☐ $10 - 2 =$ ☐

$2 + 9 =$ ☐ $12 - 5 =$ ☐ $9 \times 8 =$ ☐

$8 \times 5 =$ ☐ $2 \times 4 =$ ☐ $8 - 8 =$ ☐

$12 - 7 =$ ☐ $8 + 9 =$ ☐ $3 + 9 =$ ☐

$4 \times 6 =$ ☐ $9 - 1 =$ ☐ $13 - 4 =$ ☐

$1 + 2 =$ ☐ $2 + 4 =$ ☐ $5 + 5 =$ ☐

$8 \times 0 =$ ☐ $14 - 8 =$ ☐ $4 \times 2 =$ ☐

$6 + 7 =$ ☐ $1 \times 9 =$ ☐ $9 - 6 =$ ☐

$7 \times 2 =$ ☐ $6 + 3 =$ ☐ $7 \times 8 =$ ☐

$16 - 8 =$ ☐ $7 + 9 =$ ☐ $7 - 7 =$ ☐

$3 + 2 =$ ☐ $6 - 2 =$ ☐ $6 + 6 =$ ☐

$6 \times 7 =$ ☐ $9 \times 4 =$ ☐ $4 + 3 =$ ☐

$18 - 9 =$ ☐ $5 + 8 =$ ☐ $11 - 5 =$ ☐

$9 + 2 =$ ☐ $11 - 4 =$ ☐ $9 \times 3 =$ ☐

$6 - 5 =$ ☐ $5 \times 5 =$ ☐

End Time ☐ : ☐

I. Counting Test

Measure the time required for you to count from 1 to 120 aloud as fast as you can.

☐ sec.

II. Word Memorization Test

Memorize as many words as you can **within two minutes**.

case	island	sale	danger	leaf	towel
mouse	book	stone	apple	heat	vowel
dog	glass	reason	circle	gas	quiz
shelf	friend	pear	rock	wish	mask
talk	face	number	soup	year	bed

Write out as many words as you can remember **in two minutes** on the back of this page. How many words can you remember?

Number of words memorized ☐ words

Word Memorization Test Answers

III. Stroop Test

Please take the **Stroop Test** for Week 2, located on page **v** of the Appendix.

Start Time ☐ : ☐

3 + 2 = ☐

4 × 9 = ☐

3 × 6 = ☐

7 + 3 = ☐

10 − 2 = ☐

2 × 9 = ☐

5 + 3 = ☐

2 + 8 = ☐

13 − 8 = ☐

12 − 9 = ☐

6 × 9 = ☐

7 − 2 = ☐

4 + 1 = ☐

4 × 4 = ☐

11 − 6 = ☐

8 + 7 = ☐

8 − 8 = ☐

5 + 2 = ☐

9 × 0 = ☐

6 − 3 = ☐

7 + 4 = ☐

11 − 9 = ☐

5 × 2 = ☐

4 − 2 = ☐

3 × 2 = ☐

6 + 3 = ☐

14 − 7 = ☐

5 × 6 = ☐

8 + 5 = ☐

4 × 9 = ☐

8 × 9 = ☐

14 − 5 = ☐

9 + 7 = ☐

3 × 1 = ☐

4 + 7 = ☐

18 − 9 = ☐

3 + 4 = ☐

6 × 6 = ☐

15 − 7 = ☐

5 + 7 = ☐

8 − 7 = ☐

2 × 3 = ☐

9 × 5 = ☐

9 − 4 = ☐

3 × 9 = ☐

15 − 8 = ☐

6 + 6 = ☐

7 × 9 = ☐

7 + 0 = ☐

6 − 1 = ☐

$7 + 6 =$ ☐

$8 \times 5 =$ ☐

$4 + 6 =$ ☐

$7 - 1 =$ ☐

$13 - 7 =$ ☐

$6 \times 8 =$ ☐

$12 - 7 =$ ☐

$5 + 9 =$ ☐

$3 \times 4 =$ ☐

$15 - 9 =$ ☐

$5 - 0 =$ ☐

$2 + 7 =$ ☐

$8 + 9 =$ ☐

$9 \times 4 =$ ☐

$9 \times 8 =$ ☐

$10 - 3 =$ ☐

$9 + 2 =$ ☐

$9 - 7 =$ ☐

$8 + 6 =$ ☐

$5 \times 5 =$ ☐

$14 - 6 =$ ☐

$1 \times 1 =$ ☐

$10 - 1 =$ ☐

$3 + 0 =$ ☐

$5 \times 1 =$ ☐

$8 - 7 =$ ☐

$4 \times 6 =$ ☐

$7 + 5 =$ ☐

$12 - 3 =$ ☐

$8 \times 6 =$ ☐

$1 + 5 =$ ☐

$9 + 4 =$ ☐

$16 - 9 =$ ☐

$7 \times 2 =$ ☐

$6 \times 2 =$ ☐

$7 - 6 =$ ☐

$3 + 6 =$ ☐

$5 \times 3 =$ ☐

$4 + 8 =$ ☐

$2 + 1 =$ ☐

$11 - 7 =$ ☐

$9 \times 1 =$ ☐

$5 \times 4 =$ ☐

$9 + 6 =$ ☐

$6 - 5 =$ ☐

$14 - 8 =$ ☐

$3 \times 8 =$ ☐

$3 + 5 =$ ☐

$13 - 4 =$ ☐

$3 \times 6 =$ ☐

End Time ☐ : ☐

Date [ ] M [ ] D

Start Time [ ] : [ ]

$7 + 2 =$ [ ]

$11 - 5 =$ [ ]

$4 + 8 =$ [ ]

$7 \times 9 =$ [ ]

$9 - 4 =$ [ ]

$4 + 6 =$ [ ]

$6 - 2 =$ [ ]

$6 \times 6 =$ [ ]

$9 \times 2 =$ [ ]

$16 - 7 =$ [ ]

$3 + 6 =$ [ ]

$5 - 3 =$ [ ]

$5 + 9 =$ [ ]

$6 \times 8 =$ [ ]

$15 - 9 =$ [ ]

$3 \times 3 =$ [ ]

$5 \times 8 =$ [ ]

$7 \times 8 =$ [ ]

$10 - 9 =$ [ ]

$4 + 3 =$ [ ]

$8 + 9 =$ [ ]

$9 \times 3 =$ [ ]

$8 \times 6 =$ [ ]

$6 + 8 =$ [ ]

$7 - 6 =$ [ ]

$12 - 7 =$ [ ]

$5 \times 5 =$ [ ]

$5 + 3 =$ [ ]

$7 \times 6 =$ [ ]

$7 - 5 =$ [ ]

$3 + 9 =$ [ ]

$1 + 7 =$ [ ]

$10 - 1 =$ [ ]

$8 + 6 =$ [ ]

$11 - 9 =$ [ ]

$8 \times 3 =$ [ ]

$5 + 8 =$ [ ]

$13 - 8 =$ [ ]

$3 \times 7 =$ [ ]

$8 \times 8 =$ [ ]

$9 + 0 =$ [ ]

$15 - 6 =$ [ ]

$6 - 1 =$ [ ]

$6 + 6 =$ [ ]

$9 \times 7 =$ [ ]

$14 - 5 =$ [ ]

$9 - 8 =$ [ ]

$3 + 4 =$ [ ]

$1 \times 6 =$ [ ]

$4 + 7 =$ [ ]

$7 - 3 =$ [   ] $9 + 2 =$ [   ] $3 \times 9 =$ [   ]

$8 + 4 =$ [   ] $6 \times 5 =$ [   ] $16 - 9 =$ [   ]

$11 - 4 =$ [   ] $8 - 2 =$ [   ] $1 + 9 =$ [   ]

$4 \times 2 =$ [   ] $1 + 4 =$ [   ] $1 \times 2 =$ [   ]

$5 \times 7 =$ [   ] $12 - 5 =$ [   ] $11 - 7 =$ [   ]

$9 + 5 =$ [   ] $4 + 9 =$ [   ] $9 \times 8 =$ [   ]

$8 \times 7 =$ [   ] $4 \times 6 =$ [   ] $7 + 8 =$ [   ]

$12 - 3 =$ [   ] $5 + 1 =$ [   ] $5 + 4 =$ [   ]

$8 + 0 =$ [   ] $7 - 1 =$ [   ] $13 - 7 =$ [   ]

$4 \times 7 =$ [   ] $17 - 8 =$ [   ] $3 + 1 =$ [   ]

$6 + 7 =$ [   ] $8 \times 5 =$ [   ] $9 \times 9 =$ [   ]

$13 - 4 =$ [   ] $9 - 2 =$ [   ] $8 + 4 =$ [   ]

$2 \times 9 =$ [   ] $1 + 6 =$ [   ] $9 - 7 =$ [   ]

$11 - 8 =$ [   ] $14 - 6 =$ [   ] $7 \times 5 =$ [   ]

$3 \times 6 =$ [   ] $4 + 8 =$ [   ] $4 - 4 =$ [   ]

$7 + 6 =$ [   ] $7 + 9 =$ [   ] $7 \times 4 =$ [   ]

$15 - 7 =$ [   ] $0 \times 7 =$ [   ]

End Time [   ] : [   ]

Start Time ☐ : ☐

$9 \times 9 =$ ☐

$4 + 6 =$ ☐

$10 - 3 =$ ☐

$11 - 2 =$ ☐

$7 - 3 =$ ☐

$4 \times 4 =$ ☐

$7 + 8 =$ ☐

$4 \times 0 =$ ☐

$9 + 5 =$ ☐

$8 \times 6 =$ ☐

$12 - 8 =$ ☐

$8 - 5 =$ ☐

$2 \times 5 =$ ☐

$3 + 1 =$ ☐

$2 \times 4 =$ ☐

$11 - 8 =$ ☐

$9 \times 7 =$ ☐

$8 + 3 =$ ☐

$6 + 2 =$ ☐

$1 - 1 =$ ☐

$12 - 4 =$ ☐

$3 \times 2 =$ ☐

$7 + 7 =$ ☐

$9 \times 8 =$ ☐

$8 + 5 =$ ☐

$5 \times 6 =$ ☐

$5 + 0 =$ ☐

$6 - 3 =$ ☐

$15 - 6 =$ ☐

$5 + 7 =$ ☐

$2 + 6 =$ ☐

$8 + 1 =$ ☐

$5 \times 3 =$ ☐

$4 \times 5 =$ ☐

$9 \times 5 =$ ☐

$16 - 7 =$ ☐

$14 - 8 =$ ☐

$6 + 3 =$ ☐

$9 - 8 =$ ☐

$4 + 4 =$ ☐

$1 \times 4 =$ ☐

$4 + 8 =$ ☐

$2 \times 9 =$ ☐

$12 - 9 =$ ☐

$6 \times 7 =$ ☐

$7 - 2 =$ ☐

$9 + 4 =$ ☐

$9 - 1 =$ ☐

$2 + 8 =$ ☐

$12 - 3 =$ ☐

$11 - 5 =$ [ ] 　$8 \times 9 =$ [ ] 　$7 - 4 =$ [ ]

$4 \times 9 =$ [ ] 　$13 - 5 =$ [ ] 　$9 \times 2 =$ [ ]

$7 + 3 =$ [ ] 　$1 + 1 =$ [ ] 　$2 \times 3 =$ [ ]

$6 + 0 =$ [ ] 　$11 - 3 =$ [ ] 　$4 + 2 =$ [ ]

$17 - 9 =$ [ ] 　$2 \times 7 =$ [ ] 　$5 \times 5 =$ [ ]

$6 + 8 =$ [ ] 　$5 + 5 =$ [ ] 　$6 + 4 =$ [ ]

$1 \times 5 =$ [ ] 　$8 - 4 =$ [ ] 　$7 \times 9 =$ [ ]

$9 - 3 =$ [ ] 　$5 \times 4 =$ [ ] 　$12 - 6 =$ [ ]

$8 + 4 =$ [ ] 　$3 \times 6 =$ [ ] 　$7 + 5 =$ [ ]

$6 \times 2 =$ [ ] 　$10 - 6 =$ [ ] 　$4 \times 7 =$ [ ]

$10 - 1 =$ [ ] 　$3 + 2 =$ [ ] 　$2 \times 0 =$ [ ]

$3 + 4 =$ [ ] 　$8 + 9 =$ [ ] 　$14 - 9 =$ [ ]

$8 \times 8 =$ [ ] 　$9 - 5 =$ [ ] 　$6 + 7 =$ [ ]

$8 + 7 =$ [ ] 　$9 + 7 =$ [ ] 　$6 - 3 =$ [ ]

$10 - 9 =$ [ ] 　$15 - 8 =$ [ ] 　$5 \times 7 =$ [ ]

$6 \times 8 =$ [ ] 　$7 \times 3 =$ [ ] 　$13 - 8 =$ [ ]

$2 + 2 =$ [ ] 　$8 - 0 =$ [ ]

End Time [ ] : [ ]

42

Date ☐ M ☐ D

Start Time ☐ : ☐

$4 + 7 =$ ☐

$2 \times 8 =$ ☐

$2 + 6 =$ ☐

$6 + 8 =$ ☐

$17 - 8 =$ ☐

$7 \times 2 =$ ☐

$14 - 8 =$ ☐

$6 + 5 =$ ☐

$16 - 9 =$ ☐

$1 \times 6 =$ ☐

$9 - 6 =$ ☐

$5 + 5 =$ ☐

$9 + 3 =$ ☐

$3 \times 4 =$ ☐

$9 - 1 =$ ☐

$9 \times 9 =$ ☐

$15 - 7 =$ ☐

$9 \times 7 =$ ☐

$5 - 5 =$ ☐

$5 + 0 =$ ☐

$11 - 8 =$ ☐

$5 + 1 =$ ☐

$3 - 1 =$ ☐

$3 + 4 =$ ☐

$0 \times 3 =$ ☐

$5 + 9 =$ ☐

$10 - 2 =$ ☐

$10 - 8 =$ ☐

$2 \times 6 =$ ☐

$4 \times 7 =$ ☐

$7 + 8 =$ ☐

$14 - 6 =$ ☐

$1 + 0 =$ ☐

$8 \times 7 =$ ☐

$3 \times 3 =$ ☐

$8 - 7 =$ ☐

$9 \times 3 =$ ☐

$7 - 5 =$ ☐

$12 - 3 =$ ☐

$6 + 3 =$ ☐

$7 + 9 =$ ☐

$8 \times 6 =$ ☐

$7 - 7 =$ ☐

$6 \times 9 =$ ☐

$5 \times 7 =$ ☐

$8 + 6 =$ ☐

$17 - 9 =$ ☐

$2 + 9 =$ ☐

$4 \times 3 =$ ☐

$7 + 1 =$ ☐

$17 - 8 =$ ☐ $7 - 1 =$ ☐ $5 + 7 =$ ☐

$9 \times 2 =$ ☐ $4 \times 6 =$ ☐ $5 \times 9 =$ ☐

$8 - 3 =$ ☐ $9 + 2 =$ ☐ $10 - 4 =$ ☐

$4 + 9 =$ ☐ $7 \times 8 =$ ☐ $2 + 2 =$ ☐

$5 \times 3 =$ ☐ $13 - 5 =$ ☐ $4 \times 9 =$ ☐

$16 - 7 =$ ☐ $1 + 5 =$ ☐ $8 + 5 =$ ☐

$5 \times 6 =$ ☐ $3 \times 9 =$ ☐ $8 \times 9 =$ ☐

$4 + 8 =$ ☐ $8 + 4 =$ ☐ $7 - 2 =$ ☐

$11 - 6 =$ ☐ $12 - 7 =$ ☐ $8 + 9 =$ ☐

$4 - 3 =$ ☐ $2 \times 9 =$ ☐ $6 \times 8 =$ ☐

$8 \times 4 =$ ☐ $12 - 4 =$ ☐ $8 - 2 =$ ☐

$1 + 7 =$ ☐ $5 + 3 =$ ☐ $3 \times 8 =$ ☐

$6 + 4 =$ ☐ $3 + 7 =$ ☐ $2 + 4 =$ ☐

$7 \times 1 =$ ☐ $8 \times 2 =$ ☐ $11 - 9 =$ ☐

$6 + 2 =$ ☐ $8 \times 8 =$ ☐ $7 + 7 =$ ☐

$13 - 7 =$ ☐ $15 - 7 =$ ☐ $4 \times 8 =$ ☐

$9 - 0 =$ ☐ $7 + 6 =$ ☐

End Time ☐ : ☐

Start Time ⬜ : ⬜

5 + 2 = ⬜

7 × 3 = ⬜

12 − 8 = ⬜

3 + 9 = ⬜

3 − 3 = ⬜

2 + 4 = ⬜

2 × 5 = ⬜

17 − 9 = ⬜

1 × 1 = ⬜

1 + 4 = ⬜

12 − 3 = ⬜

9 − 8 = ⬜

8 + 8 = ⬜

10 − 4 = ⬜

5 × 9 = ⬜

3 + 3 = ⬜

6 + 6 = ⬜

8 − 0 = ⬜

3 + 6 = ⬜

3 × 8 = ⬜

5 × 7 = ⬜

5 + 6 = ⬜

6 × 0 = ⬜

12 − 9 = ⬜

7 + 9 = ⬜

1 − 1 = ⬜

4 × 9 = ⬜

15 − 9 = ⬜

3 − 2 = ⬜

9 × 8 = ⬜

4 + 9 = ⬜

6 × 5 = ⬜

14 − 9 = ⬜

11 − 3 = ⬜

8 × 5 = ⬜

9 + 5 = ⬜

2 × 3 = ⬜

9 − 1 = ⬜

4 + 5 = ⬜

5 + 7 = ⬜

7 × 6 = ⬜

11 − 7 = ⬜

7 + 2 = ⬜

6 + 5 = ⬜

10 − 1 = ⬜

9 × 7 = ⬜

8 − 6 = ⬜

7 × 4 = ⬜

4 × 4 = ⬜

8 + 6 = ⬜

$11 - 2 =$ [   ]

$4 + 7 =$ [   ]

$6 \times 4 =$ [   ]

$13 - 7 =$ [   ]

$9 \times 4 =$ [   ]

$9 + 8 =$ [   ]

$7 - 6 =$ [   ]

$5 + 4 =$ [   ]

$12 - 6 =$ [   ]

$6 \times 6 =$ [   ]

$3 + 5 =$ [   ]

$9 + 4 =$ [   ]

$4 - 2 =$ [   ]

$3 \times 9 =$ [   ]

$5 + 8 =$ [   ]

$13 - 6 =$ [   ]

$7 - 5 =$ [   ]

$3 \times 3 =$ [   ]

$7 + 6 =$ [   ]

$10 - 2 =$ [   ]

$3 \times 5 =$ [   ]

$3 - 1 =$ [   ]

$4 + 6 =$ [   ]

$17 - 8 =$ [   ]

$6 + 9 =$ [   ]

$5 \times 0 =$ [   ]

$9 - 2 =$ [   ]

$9 \times 1 =$ [   ]

$4 \times 6 =$ [   ]

$8 + 9 =$ [   ]

$3 + 4 =$ [   ]

$15 - 8 =$ [   ]

$3 \times 2 =$ [   ]

$7 \times 8 =$ [   ]

$2 + 7 =$ [   ]

$10 - 5 =$ [   ]

$9 \times 6 =$ [   ]

$5 + 5 =$ [   ]

$9 \times 6 =$ [   ]

$13 - 4 =$ [   ]

$8 \times 2 =$ [   ]

$2 + 0 =$ [   ]

$4 \times 3 =$ [   ]

$7 + 8 =$ [   ]

$6 \times 6 =$ [   ]

$16 - 8 =$ [   ]

$4 + 1 =$ [   ]

$5 \times 8 =$ [   ]

$18 - 9 =$ [   ]

$8 + 3 =$ [   ]

End Time [ ] : [ ]

I. Counting Test

Measure the time required for you to count from 1 to 120 aloud as fast as you can.

☐ sec.

II. Word Memorization Test

Memorize as many words as you can **within two minutes**.

bread	scale	change	lake	head	moon
factor	deer	watch	ship	boy	grape
table	road	plastic	ice	joy	noun
sky	bell	level	curtain	piece	king
food	teacher	ear	farmer	surface	address

Write out as many words as you can remember **in two minutes** on the back of this page. How many words can you remember?

Number of words memorized ☐ words

47

Word Memorization Test Answers

III. Stroop Test

Please take the **Stroop Test** for Week 3, located on page **vi** of the Appendix.

Day 16

Start Time ☐ : ☐

3 + 2 =

7 − 7 =

3 × 8 =

15 − 8 =

4 × 9 =

3 + 9 =

8 − 4 =

1 × 5 =

2 × 6 =

12 − 5 =

7 × 9 =

2 + 8 =

8 × 4 =

5 + 0 =

11 − 6 =

5 + 8 =

4 × 7 =

11 − 3 =

2 + 4 =

1 + 9 =

14 − 6 =

8 × 2 =

9 + 1 =

6 − 1 =

7 + 9 =

8 − 5 =

6 × 4 =

6 + 6 =

10 − 1 =

4 × 3 =

6 × 6 =

4 + 0 =

7 − 3 =

8 + 1 =

0 × 9 =

8 − 7 =

9 × 4 =

4 + 8 =

8 + 7 =

3 × 5 =

15 − 7 =

9 + 3 =

10 − 2 =

9 − 6 =

9 × 9 =

12 − 9 =

7 + 2 =

7 × 6 =

17 − 8 =

4 + 7 =

$7 - 4 =$ [ ]

$5 \times 9 =$ [ ]

$8 + 5 =$ [ ]

$15 - 9 =$ [ ]

$1 \times 7 =$ [ ]

$11 - 5 =$ [ ]

$8 + 0 =$ [ ]

$14 - 5 =$ [ ]

$4 - 4 =$ [ ]

$5 \times 2 =$ [ ]

$5 + 5 =$ [ ]

$12 - 7 =$ [ ]

$6 \times 3 =$ [ ]

$4 + 3 =$ [ ]

$13 - 7 =$ [ ]

$4 + 5 =$ [ ]

$6 \times 9 =$ [ ]

$3 \times 3 =$ [ ]

$9 - 8 =$ [ ]

$6 + 1 =$ [ ]

$4 \times 4 =$ [ ]

$7 + 6 =$ [ ]

$3 \times 4 =$ [ ]

$11 - 8 =$ [ ]

$4 + 4 =$ [ ]

$9 \times 1 =$ [ ]

$4 + 9 =$ [ ]

$14 - 8 =$ [ ]

$9 \times 7 =$ [ ]

$8 - 5 =$ [ ]

$7 + 1 =$ [ ]

$16 - 7 =$ [ ]

$7 \times 5 =$ [ ]

$8 + 6 =$ [ ]

$3 + 6 =$ [ ]

$8 \times 5 =$ [ ]

$9 + 6 =$ [ ]

$6 - 2 =$ [ ]

$14 - 7 =$ [ ]

$5 + 5 =$ [ ]

$3 \times 7 =$ [ ]

$6 + 5 =$ [ ]

$4 \times 8 =$ [ ]

$7 + 8 =$ [ ]

$5 - 4 =$ [ ]

$10 - 6 =$ [ ]

$9 + 2 =$ [ ]

$8 \times 6 =$ [ ]

$7 \times 2 =$ [ ]

$10 - 4 =$ [ ]

End Time [ ] : [ ]

Start Time ☐ : ☐

$9 \times 7 =$ ☐

$3 + 6 =$ ☐

$15 - 8 =$ ☐

$8 + 7 =$ ☐

$5 \times 6 =$ ☐

$6 \times 2 =$ ☐

$5 + 5 =$ ☐

$7 - 4 =$ ☐

$2 \times 7 =$ ☐

$14 - 8 =$ ☐

$1 + 3 =$ ☐

$7 \times 4 =$ ☐

$6 + 5 =$ ☐

$11 - 9 =$ ☐

$6 + 3 =$ ☐

$7 \times 7 =$ ☐

$11 - 4 =$ ☐

$9 + 7 =$ ☐

$8 \times 6 =$ ☐

$4 + 7 =$ ☐

$13 - 5 =$ ☐

$2 \times 8 =$ ☐

$3 + 5 =$ ☐

$4 \times 6 =$ ☐

$7 + 8 =$ ☐

$8 - 6 =$ ☐

$12 - 4 =$ ☐

$9 \times 8 =$ ☐

$10 - 5 =$ ☐

$6 - 3 =$ ☐

$5 + 1 =$ ☐

$9 \times 3 =$ ☐

$2 + 9 =$ ☐

$7 \times 2 =$ ☐

$4 + 4 =$ ☐

$13 - 6 =$ ☐

$1 + 9 =$ ☐

$0 \times 6 =$ ☐

$8 - 7 =$ ☐

$8 + 3 =$ ☐

$3 - 3 =$ ☐

$3 \times 5 =$ ☐

$9 \times 1 =$ ☐

$5 + 3 =$ ☐

$12 - 8 =$ ☐

$6 + 9 =$ ☐

$5 \times 5 =$ ☐

$9 - 6 =$ ☐

$14 - 6 =$ ☐

$3 \times 6 =$ ☐

4 + 7 = ☐	1 × 2 = ☐	12 − 4 = ☐
6 × 9 = ☐	14 − 5 = ☐	8 + 4 = ☐
3 + 4 = ☐	7 + 3 = ☐	6 − 3 = ☐
9 − 3 = ☐	5 × 7 = ☐	5 × 3 = ☐
3 − 0 = ☐	9 × 4 = ☐	3 − 1 = ☐
9 + 4 = ☐	10 − 3 = ☐	9 + 9 = ☐
3 × 9 = ☐	3 + 8 = ☐	8 × 3 = ☐
5 − 2 = ☐	11 − 5 = ☐	11 − 3 = ☐
4 + 5 = ☐	8 + 1 = ☐	6 + 2 = ☐
5 × 4 = ☐	7 × 5 = ☐	12 − 8 = ☐
16 − 8 = ☐	7 × 6 = ☐	6 × 7 = ☐
9 − 7 = ☐	8 + 6 = ☐	7 + 6 = ☐
1 + 2 = ☐	6 − 2 = ☐	8 × 4 = ☐
12 − 9 = ☐	2 + 2 = ☐	13 − 4 = ☐
5 + 7 = ☐	8 × 5 = ☐	9 × 2 = ☐
4 × 5 = ☐	10 − 5 = ☐	4 + 6 = ☐
8 + 9 = ☐	3 × 8 = ☐	

End Time ☐ : ☐

Day 18

Start Time ☐ : ☐

$4 \times 7 =$ ☐ $16 - 7 =$ ☐

$14 - 7 =$ ☐ $7 + 4 =$ ☐ $7 - 3 =$ ☐

$7 + 7 =$ ☐ $5 - 1 =$ ☐ $2 \times 2 =$ ☐

$6 \times 4 =$ ☐ $16 - 8 =$ ☐ $9 + 6 =$ ☐

$9 \times 7 =$ ☐ $3 + 6 =$ ☐ $9 - 4 =$ ☐

$2 + 6 =$ ☐ $3 \times 3 =$ ☐ $7 \times 4 =$ ☐

$14 - 9 =$ ☐ $4 + 8 =$ ☐ $15 - 6 =$ ☐

$5 \times 3 =$ ☐ $7 - 0 =$ ☐ $6 + 7 =$ ☐

$8 - 3 =$ ☐ $9 \times 6 =$ ☐ $9 \times 5 =$ ☐

$8 + 1 =$ ☐ $11 - 2 =$ ☐ $3 + 5 =$ ☐

$4 + 9 =$ ☐ $6 \times 5 =$ ☐ $8 + 6 =$ ☐

$7 \times 2 =$ ☐ $7 + 5 =$ ☐ $9 \times 1 =$ ☐

$12 - 5 =$ ☐ $2 \times 7 =$ ☐ $17 - 8 =$ ☐

$1 + 0 =$ ☐ $6 + 3 =$ ☐ $8 \times 4 =$ ☐

$4 - 4 =$ ☐ $10 - 1 =$ ☐ $3 + 7 =$ ☐

$3 \times 6 =$ ☐ $5 + 2 =$ ☐ $5 - 4 =$ ☐

$9 + 3 =$ ☐ $14 - 6 =$ ☐ $8 \times 2 =$ ☐

$8 \times 9 =$ ☐

$11 - 5 =$ ☐

$8 - 6 =$ ☐

$1 + 9 =$ ☐

$7 \times 8 =$ ☐

$2 + 5 =$ ☐

$9 - 8 =$ ☐

$8 \times 1 =$ ☐

$15 - 7 =$ ☐

$8 \times 6 =$ ☐

$8 + 3 =$ ☐

$7 - 2 =$ ☐

$6 + 0 =$ ☐

$9 + 5 =$ ☐

$10 - 3 =$ ☐

$6 \times 6 =$ ☐

$16 - 9 =$ ☐

$3 + 2 =$ ☐

$6 + 5 =$ ☐

$6 \times 3 =$ ☐

$9 - 9 =$ ☐

$8 + 8 =$ ☐

$1 \times 3 =$ ☐

$4 + 7 =$ ☐

$13 - 9 =$ ☐

$2 + 7 =$ ☐

$8 \times 7 =$ ☐

$2 \times 6 =$ ☐

$14 - 8 =$ ☐

$9 + 4 =$ ☐

$5 + 1 =$ ☐

$7 \times 7 =$ ☐

$13 - 4 =$ ☐

$5 - 3 =$ ☐

$11 - 4 =$ ☐

$2 \times 5 =$ ☐

$5 + 6 =$ ☐

$7 + 1 =$ ☐

$7 \times 9 =$ ☐

$7 + 8 =$ ☐

$10 - 8 =$ ☐

$9 - 7 =$ ☐

$4 + 6 =$ ☐

$3 \times 8 =$ ☐

$17 - 9 =$ ☐

$6 \times 5 =$ ☐

$9 \times 9 =$ ☐

$5 + 9 =$ ☐

$10 - 6 =$ ☐

$4 \times 8 =$ ☐

End Time ☐ : ☐

Day 19

Start Time ☐ : ☐

$3 + 8 =$ ☐

$7 + 0 =$ ☐

$1 \times 6 =$ ☐

$6 + 4 =$ ☐

$9 \times 8 =$ ☐

$5 - 5 =$ ☐

$16 - 8 =$ ☐

$3 \times 6 =$ ☐

$13 - 9 =$ ☐

$5 + 6 =$ ☐

$4 \times 6 =$ ☐

$4 \times 3 =$ ☐

$1 + 5 =$ ☐

$8 \times 2 =$ ☐

$6 + 6 =$ ☐

$5 - 3 =$ ☐

$3 \times 9 =$ ☐

$10 - 1 =$ ☐

$9 + 8 =$ ☐

$6 - 6 =$ ☐

$2 \times 3 =$ ☐

$14 - 5 =$ ☐

$5 + 3 =$ ☐

$8 + 5 =$ ☐

$6 - 3 =$ ☐

$9 \times 3 =$ ☐

$16 - 9 =$ ☐

$1 \times 7 =$ ☐

$9 + 9 =$ ☐

$8 - 2 =$ ☐

$2 + 4 =$ ☐

$12 - 5 =$ ☐

$6 \times 6 =$ ☐

$9 + 2 =$ ☐

$9 \times 2 =$ ☐

$3 + 4 =$ ☐

$12 - 6 =$ ☐

$5 + 9 =$ ☐

$7 \times 5 =$ ☐

$3 - 2 =$ ☐

$13 - 5 =$ ☐

$8 + 1 =$ ☐

$13 - 8 =$ ☐

$7 \times 9 =$ ☐

$9 \times 4 =$ ☐

$9 - 7 =$ ☐

$11 - 4 =$ ☐

$8 \times 5 =$ ☐

$3 + 2 =$ ☐

$7 + 9 =$ ☐

$2 - 1 =$ [ ]　　　$5 \times 5 =$ [ ]　　　$14 - 9 =$ [ ]

$9 + 0 =$ [ ]　　　$9 + 1 =$ [ ]　　　$6 \times 4 =$ [ ]

$9 \times 5 =$ [ ]　　　$18 - 9 =$ [ ]　　　$8 + 2 =$ [ ]

$10 - 6 =$ [ ]　　　$8 \times 3 =$ [ ]　　　$5 - 2 =$ [ ]

$3 \times 2 =$ [ ]　　　$17 - 8 =$ [ ]　　　$5 \times 8 =$ [ ]

$7 + 2 =$ [ ]　　　$8 + 5 =$ [ ]　　　$11 - 8 =$ [ ]

$2 \times 1 =$ [ ]　　　$4 + 2 =$ [ ]　　　$9 - 5 =$ [ ]

$4 + 9 =$ [ ]　　　$8 - 3 =$ [ ]　　　$5 + 8 =$ [ ]

$14 - 6 =$ [ ]　　　$5 \times 9 =$ [ ]　　　$2 \times 5 =$ [ ]

$3 \times 3 =$ [ ]　　　$2 + 9 =$ [ ]　　　$12 - 9 =$ [ ]

$3 + 5 =$ [ ]　　　$7 - 3 =$ [ ]　　　$7 \times 6 =$ [ ]

$4 + 6 =$ [ ]　　　$6 \times 8 =$ [ ]　　　$5 + 4 =$ [ ]

$15 - 7 =$ [ ]　　　$3 + 1 =$ [ ]　　　$7 + 5 =$ [ ]

$6 \times 5 =$ [ ]　　　$10 - 3 =$ [ ]　　　$2 \times 7 =$ [ ]

$12 - 8 =$ [ ]　　　$8 + 9 =$ [ ]　　　$10 - 5 =$ [ ]

$4 \times 9 =$ [ ]　　　$6 - 4 =$ [ ]　　　$4 + 8 =$ [ ]

$3 + 9 =$ [ ]　　　$4 \times 7 =$ [ ]

End Time [ ] : [ ]

Day 20

Date ☐ M ☐ D

Start Time ☐ : ☐

$4 - 1 =$ ☐

$6 + 2 =$ ☐

$5 + 5 =$ ☐

$3 \times 8 =$ ☐

$9 - 5 =$ ☐

$4 \times 0 =$ ☐

$11 - 6 =$ ☐

$8 + 7 =$ ☐

$2 \times 5 =$ ☐

$4 \times 3 =$ ☐

$18 - 9 =$ ☐

$5 - 3 =$ ☐

$9 \times 4 =$ ☐

$3 + 9 =$ ☐

$12 - 8 =$ ☐

$9 \times 7 =$ ☐

$13 - 5 =$ ☐

$7 \times 3 =$ ☐

$4 + 8 =$ ☐

$5 \times 3 =$ ☐

$1 \times 8 =$ ☐

$6 + 9 =$ ☐

$5 - 2 =$ ☐

$6 \times 9 =$ ☐

$10 - 6 =$ ☐

$8 + 1 =$ ☐

$4 + 7 =$ ☐

$16 - 9 =$ ☐

$9 \times 3 =$ ☐

$6 - 0 =$ ☐

$2 \times 4 =$ ☐

$2 \times 7 =$ ☐

$2 + 1 =$ ☐

$8 + 6 =$ ☐

$5 + 4 =$ ☐

$9 \times 5 =$ ☐

$13 - 6 =$ ☐

$3 + 7 =$ ☐

$8 - 7 =$ ☐

$6 \times 3 =$ ☐

$2 + 7 =$ ☐

$10 - 9 =$ ☐

$4 \times 8 =$ ☐

$11 - 4 =$ ☐

$7 + 9 =$ ☐

$6 - 5 =$ ☐

$8 + 8 =$ ☐

$4 + 3 =$ ☐

$6 \times 5 =$ ☐

$15 - 8 =$ ☐

2 + 9 = ☐

13 − 9 = ☐

4 × 6 = ☐

5 − 3 = ☐

8 × 4 = ☐

9 + 6 = ☐

12 − 9 = ☐

5 + 7 = ☐

3 × 4 = ☐

6 − 2 = ☐

2 × 9 = ☐

8 − 5 = ☐

4 + 6 = ☐

3 × 2 = ☐

8 × 9 = ☐

3 + 5 = ☐

17 − 8 = ☐

4 × 3 = ☐

5 + 1 = ☐

18 − 9 = ☐

6 + 5 = ☐

6 × 8 = ☐

3 × 7 = ☐

1 + 2 = ☐

14 − 7 = ☐

9 + 5 = ☐

2 × 6 = ☐

7 × 4 = ☐

12 − 6 = ☐

2 + 4 = ☐

8 × 6 = ☐

14 − 9 = ☐

9 + 7 = ☐

9 − 5 = ☐

10 − 8 = ☐

5 + 6 = ☐

7 × 9 = ☐

12 − 5 = ☐

4 × 2 = ☐

6 + 7 = ☐

8 − 8 = ☐

1 + 6 = ☐

10 − 2 = ☐

9 + 0 = ☐

11 − 5 = ☐

9 + 8 = ☐

9 − 3 = ☐

4 × 7 = ☐

8 + 2 = ☐

6 × 7 = ☐

End Time ☐ : ☐

I. Counting Test

Measure the time required for you to count from 1 to 120 aloud as fast as you can.

☐ sec.

II. Word Memorization Test

Memorize as many words as you can **within two minutes**.

diet	code	spring	eel	floor	heart
paint	magnet	water	tomato	seal	gold
base	crown	nothing	insect	type	street
line	song	project	tarp	orange	actor
world	member	region	sum	ride	purse

Write out as many words as you can remember **in two minutes** on the back of this page. How many words can you remember?

Number of words memorized ☐ words

Word Memorization Test Answers

III. Stroop Test

Please take the **Stroop Test** for Week 4, located on page **vii** of the Appendix.

Date ☐ M ☐ D

Start Time ☐ : ☐

$13 - 9 =$ ☐

$1 + 2 =$ ☐

$8 + 8 =$ ☐

$12 - 8 =$ ☐

$9 \times 4 =$ ☐

$7 + 8 =$ ☐

$5 - 3 =$ ☐

$4 + 6 =$ ☐

$6 - 2 =$ ☐

$7 \times 3 =$ ☐

$8 + 4 =$ ☐

$17 - 9 =$ ☐

$9 \times 6 =$ ☐

$6 \times 5 =$ ☐

$2 + 7 =$ ☐

$8 - 5 =$ ☐

$4 + 0 =$ ☐

$7 \times 4 =$ ☐

$9 - 5 =$ ☐

$4 \times 5 =$ ☐

$8 + 7 =$ ☐

$4 + 4 =$ ☐

$8 \times 5 =$ ☐

$14 - 6 =$ ☐

$9 + 7 =$ ☐

$2 \times 9 =$ ☐

$5 - 5 =$ ☐

$4 \times 2 =$ ☐

$13 - 9 =$ ☐

$3 + 6 =$ ☐

$7 \times 9 =$ ☐

$12 - 5 =$ ☐

$6 + 8 =$ ☐

$9 \times 9 =$ ☐

$5 + 2 =$ ☐

$8 - 3 =$ ☐

$6 \times 4 =$ ☐

$15 - 7 =$ ☐

$3 \times 5 =$ ☐

$7 + 6 =$ ☐

$6 - 5 =$ ☐

$5 \times 4 =$ ☐

$8 \times 4 =$ ☐

$10 - 1 =$ ☐

$1 \times 9 =$ ☐

$5 + 7 =$ ☐

$7 \times 7 =$ ☐

$2 + 5 =$ ☐

$11 - 3 =$ ☐

$9 + 1 =$ ☐

2 × 4 = ☐	3 + 0 = ☐	8 − 7 = ☐
7 − 2 = ☐	7 × 8 = ☐	5 × 6 = ☐
1 + 4 = ☐	8 + 6 = ☐	4 + 6 = ☐
9 × 1 = ☐	9 − 6 = ☐	13 − 5 = ☐
7 + 9 = ☐	12 − 4 = ☐	9 × 5 = ☐
4 × 8 = ☐	9 + 5 = ☐	13 − 7 = ☐
13 − 4 = ☐	8 × 2 = ☐	4 + 5 = ☐
2 + 2 = ☐	6 + 8 = ☐	2 × 7 = ☐
4 × 9 = ☐	3 × 9 = ☐	8 − 8 = ☐
5 + 9 = ☐	6 + 4 = ☐	9 × 2 = ☐
12 − 6 = ☐	9 − 1 = ☐	8 + 2 = ☐
5 × 7 = ☐	12 − 9 = ☐	10 − 8 = ☐
3 − 2 = ☐	9 + 3 = ☐	6 × 8 = ☐
3 + 5 = ☐	6 × 7 = ☐	6 + 2 = ☐
10 − 4 = ☐	5 × 3 = ☐	12 − 7 = ☐
2 × 3 = ☐	14 − 7 = ☐	9 + 6 = ☐
7 + 3 = ☐	6 × 3 = ☐	

End Time ☐ : ☐

Start Time ☐ : ☐

$5 \times 7 =$ ☐

$15 - 7 =$ ☐

$6 + 6 =$ ☐

$0 + 5 =$ ☐

$6 \times 8 =$ ☐

$6 \times 3 =$ ☐

$13 - 5 =$ ☐

$2 + 4 =$ ☐

$3 + 9 =$ ☐

$6 + 5 =$ ☐

$14 - 8 =$ ☐

$11 - 6 =$ ☐

$8 \times 3 =$ ☐

$3 + 8 =$ ☐

$4 \times 9 =$ ☐

$9 - 1 =$ ☐

$9 \times 9 =$ ☐

$1 + 7 =$ ☐

$9 + 9 =$ ☐

$4 \times 7 =$ ☐

$3 \times 7 =$ ☐

$8 - 2 =$ ☐

$9 + 2 =$ ☐

$1 + 9 =$ ☐

$9 \times 8 =$ ☐

$9 - 8 =$ ☐

$9 - 6 =$ ☐

$3 \times 6 =$ ☐

$5 \times 2 =$ ☐

$13 - 4 =$ ☐

$5 + 4 =$ ☐

$13 - 8 =$ ☐

$2 \times 3 =$ ☐

$11 - 3 =$ ☐

$7 + 0 =$ ☐

$12 - 4 =$ ☐

$7 + 5 =$ ☐

$8 \times 7 =$ ☐

$7 - 2 =$ ☐

$4 \times 3 =$ ☐

$5 + 8 =$ ☐

$2 + 6 =$ ☐

$1 - 1 =$ ☐

$7 - 4 =$ ☐

$2 \times 9 =$ ☐

$10 - 9 =$ ☐

$4 + 3 =$ ☐

$6 + 7 =$ ☐

$8 \times 5 =$ ☐

$12 - 6 =$ ☐

$7 \times 2 =$ ☐ $13 - 7 =$ ☐ $8 + 9 =$ ☐

$12 - 8 =$ ☐ $4 + 8 =$ ☐ $2 \times 7 =$ ☐

$9 + 7 =$ ☐ $8 - 5 =$ ☐ $5 + 3 =$ ☐

$3 \times 8 =$ ☐ $6 \times 6 =$ ☐ $4 - 1 =$ ☐

$2 \times 6 =$ ☐ $3 - 2 =$ ☐ $11 - 2 =$ ☐

$17 - 9 =$ ☐ $5 + 5 =$ ☐ $8 + 3 =$ ☐

$5 + 6 =$ ☐ $7 \times 8 =$ ☐ $9 \times 7 =$ ☐

$13 - 5 =$ ☐ $10 - 6 =$ ☐ $8 - 4 =$ ☐

$6 + 2 =$ ☐ $7 + 2 =$ ☐ $4 + 1 =$ ☐

$16 - 8 =$ ☐ $14 - 5 =$ ☐ $5 \times 5 =$ ☐

$9 \times 4 =$ ☐ $9 \times 1 =$ ☐ $12 - 5 =$ ☐

$8 + 8 =$ ☐ $4 + 7 =$ ☐ $6 - 3 =$ ☐

$5 - 2 =$ ☐ $3 \times 0 =$ ☐ $3 + 2 =$ ☐

$3 + 6 =$ ☐ $10 - 3 =$ ☐ $11 - 8 =$ ☐

$8 \times 4 =$ ☐ $4 \times 5 =$ ☐ $6 + 4 =$ ☐

$15 - 9 =$ ☐ $9 + 7 =$ ☐ $9 \times 5 =$ ☐

$4 \times 6 =$ ☐ $7 + 6 =$ ☐

End Time ☐ : ☐

Start Time [ ] : [ ]

$8 + 6 =$ [ ]

$3 - 2 =$ [ ]

$12 - 6 =$ [ ]

$3 + 5 =$ [ ]

$2 \times 7 =$ [ ]

$7 + 7 =$ [ ]

$3 - 1 =$ [ ]

$8 \times 8 =$ [ ]

$11 - 5 =$ [ ]

$6 \times 0 =$ [ ]

$9 + 8 =$ [ ]

$1 \times 2 =$ [ ]

$2 + 6 =$ [ ]

$10 - 3 =$ [ ]

$5 + 3 =$ [ ]

$12 - 7 =$ [ ]

$14 - 8 =$ [ ]

$8 - 6 =$ [ ]

$3 \times 3 =$ [ ]

$2 + 9 =$ [ ]

$4 - 2 =$ [ ]

$7 \times 6 =$ [ ]

$15 - 7 =$ [ ]

$8 + 8 =$ [ ]

$3 \times 2 =$ [ ]

$2 + 4 =$ [ ]

$5 + 9 =$ [ ]

$9 \times 3 =$ [ ]

$12 - 8 =$ [ ]

$8 \times 6 =$ [ ]

$3 + 8 =$ [ ]

$9 - 3 =$ [ ]

$7 \times 1 =$ [ ]

$3 \times 7 =$ [ ]

$15 - 8 =$ [ ]

$6 + 4 =$ [ ]

$5 \times 2 =$ [ ]

$8 \times 4 =$ [ ]

$4 + 0 =$ [ ]

$11 - 2 =$ [ ]

$1 \times 4 =$ [ ]

$6 - 4 =$ [ ]

$1 + 4 =$ [ ]

$8 + 9 =$ [ ]

$2 \times 8 =$ [ ]

$11 - 3 =$ [ ]

$3 + 2 =$ [ ]

$8 - 7 =$ [ ]

$9 \times 2 =$ [ ]

$4 + 7 =$ [ ]

$2 + 7 =$ ☐

$7 + 8 =$ ☐

$6 \times 3 =$ ☐

$5 - 1 =$ ☐

$7 + 4 =$ ☐

$4 \times 9 =$ ☐

$9 + 6 =$ ☐

$11 - 7 =$ ☐

$2 + 3 =$ ☐

$7 \times 8 =$ ☐

$3 \times 1 =$ ☐

$10 - 6 =$ ☐

$8 + 4 =$ ☐

$5 + 1 =$ ☐

$5 \times 0 =$ ☐

$11 - 9 =$ ☐

$1 - 1 =$ ☐

$15 - 9 =$ ☐

$5 \times 9 =$ ☐

$9 + 7 =$ ☐

$3 + 3 =$ ☐

$6 \times 1 =$ ☐

$9 + 1 =$ ☐

$10 - 2 =$ ☐

$7 - 5 =$ ☐

$8 + 2 =$ ☐

$7 \times 3 =$ ☐

$10 - 5 =$ ☐

$9 \times 9 =$ ☐

$3 \times 4 =$ ☐

$3 + 7 =$ ☐

$11 - 6 =$ ☐

$8 \times 9 =$ ☐

$16 - 7 =$ ☐

$6 \times 6 =$ ☐

$12 - 9 =$ ☐

$6 - 4 =$ ☐

$9 + 2 =$ ☐

$2 \times 9 =$ ☐

$5 + 2 =$ ☐

$9 - 6 =$ ☐

$5 \times 4 =$ ☐

$12 - 4 =$ ☐

$6 \times 2 =$ ☐

$9 + 4 =$ ☐

$8 - 4 =$ ☐

$4 + 2 =$ ☐

$5 + 7 =$ ☐

$16 - 8 =$ ☐

$12 - 7 =$ ☐

End Time ☐ : ☐

66

Date ☐ M ☐ D

Start Time ☐ : ☐

$14 - 7 =$ ☐

$3 + 9 =$ ☐

$8 - 3 =$ ☐

$5 \times 3 =$ ☐

$10 - 7 =$ ☐

$7 + 1 =$ ☐

$9 + 2 =$ ☐

$9 - 4 =$ ☐

$8 \times 3 =$ ☐

$12 - 8 =$ ☐

$1 \times 3 =$ ☐

$4 + 9 =$ ☐

$8 - 7 =$ ☐

$8 + 1 =$ ☐

$15 - 6 =$ ☐

$3 \times 2 =$ ☐

$5 + 8 =$ ☐

$2 \times 8 =$ ☐

$9 + 0 =$ ☐

$16 - 8 =$ ☐

$8 + 5 =$ ☐

$5 \times 6 =$ ☐

$5 - 4 =$ ☐

$12 - 3 =$ ☐

$1 + 3 =$ ☐

$10 - 1 =$ ☐

$9 \times 8 =$ ☐

$3 \times 3 =$ ☐

$6 - 4 =$ ☐

$14 - 6 =$ ☐

$5 \times 5 =$ ☐

$3 + 4 =$ ☐

$6 + 4 =$ ☐

$9 \times 0 =$ ☐

$6 + 8 =$ ☐

$1 + 5 =$ ☐

$3 \times 7 =$ ☐

$5 + 7 =$ ☐

$9 \times 3 =$ ☐

$7 - 7 =$ ☐

$14 - 9 =$ ☐

$9 \times 6 =$ ☐

$11 - 8 =$ ☐

$7 + 3 =$ ☐

$8 \times 9 =$ ☐

$5 \times 4 =$ ☐

$2 + 2 =$ ☐

$4 \times 9 =$ ☐

$7 + 8 =$ ☐

$7 - 3 =$ ☐

$7 \times 2 =$ ☐ $12 - 7 =$ ☐ $9 - 6 =$ ☐

$8 + 6 =$ ☐ $2 \times 7 =$ ☐ $3 + 6 =$ ☐

$14 - 5 =$ ☐ $5 + 6 =$ ☐ $2 \times 4 =$ ☐

$8 \times 2 =$ ☐ $4 - 2 =$ ☐ $12 - 9 =$ ☐

$11 - 6 =$ ☐ $2 \times 3 =$ ☐ $8 \times 4 =$ ☐

$1 + 9 =$ ☐ $12 - 4 =$ ☐ $1 + 1 =$ ☐

$3 + 5 =$ ☐ $9 - 1 =$ ☐ $3 \times 1 =$ ☐

$6 - 3 =$ ☐ $6 + 5 =$ ☐ $4 + 8 =$ ☐

$7 \times 3 =$ ☐ $9 \times 7 =$ ☐ $16 - 7 =$ ☐

$9 + 4 =$ ☐ $13 - 4 =$ ☐ $2 \times 5 =$ ☐

$8 - 6 =$ ☐ $8 \times 8 =$ ☐ $1 + 6 =$ ☐

$3 \times 4 =$ ☐ $4 + 5 =$ ☐ $8 + 3 =$ ☐

$0 + 2 =$ ☐ $7 + 7 =$ ☐ $15 - 8 =$ ☐

$17 - 8 =$ ☐ $6 \times 8 =$ ☐ $6 \times 3 =$ ☐

$8 + 7 =$ ☐ $11 - 9 =$ ☐ $17 - 9 =$ ☐

$5 - 5 =$ ☐ $4 + 6 =$ ☐ $4 \times 3 =$ ☐

$1 \times 2 =$ ☐ $5 + 7 =$ ☐

End Time ☐ : ☐

Start Time ☐ : ☐

$8 \times 4 =$ ☐

$4 + 7 =$ ☐

$2 \times 4 =$ ☐

$1 \times 9 =$ ☐

$6 + 5 =$ ☐

$4 - 1 =$ ☐

$6 \times 6 =$ ☐

$11 - 6 =$ ☐

$5 + 2 =$ ☐

$9 + 2 =$ ☐

$10 - 2 =$ ☐

$3 \times 5 =$ ☐

$7 - 6 =$ ☐

$3 \times 4 =$ ☐

$4 \times 4 =$ ☐

$1 + 6 =$ ☐

$8 + 6 =$ ☐

$4 + 3 =$ ☐

$3 \times 6 =$ ☐

$15 - 7 =$ ☐

$8 + 5 =$ ☐

$6 - 4 =$ ☐

$7 \times 7 =$ ☐

$3 + 5 =$ ☐

$15 - 9 =$ ☐

$4 \times 2 =$ ☐

$14 - 5 =$ ☐

$2 + 9 =$ ☐

$9 - 8 =$ ☐

$4 + 7 =$ ☐

$3 + 4 =$ ☐

$9 \times 6 =$ ☐

$10 - 6 =$ ☐

$11 - 9 =$ ☐

$6 - 3 =$ ☐

$6 + 0 =$ ☐

$8 + 2 =$ ☐

$2 \times 9 =$ ☐

$8 - 3 =$ ☐

$6 \times 7 =$ ☐

$10 - 4 =$ ☐

$5 + 5 =$ ☐

$8 \times 3 =$ ☐

$2 + 7 =$ ☐

$14 - 8 =$ ☐

$7 - 1 =$ ☐

$3 \times 2 =$ ☐

$7 + 3 =$ ☐

$12 - 8 =$ ☐

$9 \times 8 =$ ☐

$8 \times 9 =$ ☐

$2 + 0 =$ ☐

$16 - 7 =$ ☐

$6 + 8 =$ ☐

$7 \times 2 =$ ☐

$4 \times 8 =$ ☐

$1 + 3 =$ ☐

$10 - 1 =$ ☐

$5 + 8 =$ ☐

$5 \times 9 =$ ☐

$6 \times 4 =$ ☐

$15 - 8 =$ ☐

$2 + 6 =$ ☐

$5 \times 3 =$ ☐

$12 - 6 =$ ☐

$9 + 6 =$ ☐

$9 - 9 =$ ☐

$11 - 5 =$ ☐

$5 + 6 =$ ☐

$1 \times 8 =$ ☐

$17 - 8 =$ ☐

$9 \times 4 =$ ☐

$8 + 7 =$ ☐

$5 - 0 =$ ☐

$7 + 1 =$ ☐

$14 - 9 =$ ☐

$6 + 2 =$ ☐

$12 - 5 =$ ☐

$9 + 4 =$ ☐

$6 - 4 =$ ☐

$5 \times 4 =$ ☐

$6 + 7 =$ ☐

$6 \times 9 =$ ☐

$14 - 6 =$ ☐

$8 + 3 =$ ☐

$13 - 9 =$ ☐

$4 \times 6 =$ ☐

$7 - 4 =$ ☐

$9 \times 7 =$ ☐

$6 + 4 =$ ☐

$13 - 5 =$ ☐

$9 + 8 =$ ☐

$2 \times 7 =$ ☐

$3 - 2 =$ ☐

$6 \times 8 =$ ☐

$7 - 6 =$ ☐

$5 + 9 =$ ☐

$2 \times 2 =$ ☐

$5 \times 6 =$ ☐

$3 + 6 =$ ☐

End Time ☐ : ☐

I. Counting Test

Measure the time required for you to count from 1 to 120 aloud as fast as you can.

☐ sec.

II. Word Memorization Test

Memorize as many words as you can **within two minutes**.

sail	radio	fact	day	plane	minute
lace	vision	colony	show	inch	man
corn	sleep	area	weather	girl	frame
berry	snow	rule	copy	job	neck
home	picture	onion	child	system	tail

Write out as many words as you can remember **in two minutes** on the back of this page. How many words can you remember?

Number of words memorized ☐ words

Word Memorization Test Answers

III. Stroop Test

Please take the **Stroop Test** for Week 5, located on page **viii** of the Appendix.

Start Time [ ] : [ ]

$3 \times 6 =$ [ ]

$8 - 3 =$ [ ]

$9 \times 7 =$ [ ]

$3 + 8 =$ [ ]

$7 + 0 =$ [ ]

$9 \times 2 =$ [ ]

$14 - 7 =$ [ ]

$6 + 4 =$ [ ]

$16 - 9 =$ [ ]

$6 - 5 =$ [ ]

$1 \times 3 =$ [ ]

$10 - 9 =$ [ ]

$1 + 5 =$ [ ]

$6 \times 7 =$ [ ]

$13 - 6 =$ [ ]

$9 + 9 =$ [ ]

$7 \times 1 =$ [ ]

$5 + 4 =$ [ ]

$9 - 8 =$ [ ]

$3 \times 4 =$ [ ]

$17 - 8 =$ [ ]

$8 \times 3 =$ [ ]

$6 + 6 =$ [ ]

$9 - 2 =$ [ ]

$5 \times 9 =$ [ ]

$9 \times 3 =$ [ ]

$11 - 6 =$ [ ]

$7 \times 6 =$ [ ]

$7 + 5 =$ [ ]

$5 \times 4 =$ [ ]

$1 + 7 =$ [ ]

$11 - 9 =$ [ ]

$5 + 9 =$ [ ]

$2 + 4 =$ [ ]

$10 - 2 =$ [ ]

$1 + 4 =$ [ ]

$9 + 3 =$ [ ]

$11 - 5 =$ [ ]

$3 \times 7 =$ [ ]

$4 + 9 =$ [ ]

$7 - 5 =$ [ ]

$3 + 7 =$ [ ]

$4 - 1 =$ [ ]

$6 \times 2 =$ [ ]

$7 + 4 =$ [ ]

$12 - 4 =$ [ ]

$5 \times 3 =$ [ ]

$7 \times 7 =$ [ ]

$4 + 4 =$ [ ]

$7 - 1 =$ [ ]

3 + 5 = ☐

1 × 6 = ☐

8 + 6 = ☐

4 − 2 = ☐

12 − 7 = ☐

8 + 2 = ☐

4 × 8 = ☐

1 + 9 = ☐

0 × 0 = ☐

7 + 7 = ☐

8 − 5 = ☐

15 − 7 = ☐

5 + 6 = ☐

8 × 2 = ☐

3 × 5 = ☐

10 − 1 = ☐

9 + 4 = ☐

6 − 4 = ☐

6 × 3 = ☐

7 + 8 = ☐

14 − 8 = ☐

4 × 4 = ☐

18 − 9 = ☐

3 + 1 = ☐

14 − 5 = ☐

5 − 0 = ☐

5 + 7 = ☐

6 × 1 = ☐

15 − 8 = ☐

6 × 4 = ☐

0 + 4 = ☐

10 − 7 = ☐

5 + 8 = ☐

3 × 9 = ☐

2 × 3 = ☐

9 − 3 = ☐

2 + 6 = ☐

2 × 7 = ☐

9 + 6 = ☐

4 × 9 = ☐

16 − 7 = ☐

1 + 1 = ☐

4 × 5 = ☐

6 + 9 = ☐

11 − 2 = ☐

8 × 9 = ☐

9 − 5 = ☐

8 + 0 = ☐

10 − 5 = ☐

5 × 7 = ☐

End Time ☐ : ☐

Date ☐ M ☐ D

Start Time ☐ : ☐

$2 + 2 =$ ☐

$12 - 6 =$ ☐

$7 + 3 =$ ☐

$6 \times 4 =$ ☐

$8 - 7 =$ ☐

$6 + 5 =$ ☐

$5 - 3 =$ ☐

$3 \times 5 =$ ☐

$2 \times 1 =$ ☐

$1 + 6 =$ ☐

$13 - 9 =$ ☐

$8 + 5 =$ ☐

$5 \times 9 =$ ☐

$5 - 2 =$ ☐

$12 - 8 =$ ☐

$4 \times 9 =$ ☐

$2 \times 9 =$ ☐

$3 \times 0 =$ ☐

$3 + 4 =$ ☐

$13 - 7 =$ ☐

$9 + 9 =$ ☐

$7 \times 9 =$ ☐

$4 \times 4 =$ ☐

$6 + 4 =$ ☐

$3 - 3 =$ ☐

$9 \times 8 =$ ☐

$13 - 5 =$ ☐

$5 + 4 =$ ☐

$7 \times 7 =$ ☐

$9 + 3 =$ ☐

$3 - 2 =$ ☐

$2 + 5 =$ ☐

$14 - 8 =$ ☐

$10 - 4 =$ ☐

$5 + 9 =$ ☐

$5 \times 2 =$ ☐

$4 + 8 =$ ☐

$14 - 5 =$ ☐

$8 \times 4 =$ ☐

$4 + 4 =$ ☐

$5 \times 8 =$ ☐

$2 + 8 =$ ☐

$9 - 7 =$ ☐

$10 - 3 =$ ☐

$2 \times 8 =$ ☐

$10 - 1 =$ ☐

$9 - 3 =$ ☐

$1 + 4 =$ ☐

$9 \times 3 =$ ☐

$7 + 7 =$ ☐

$15 - 7 =$ ☐ $1 + 9 =$ ☐ $6 \times 9 =$ ☐

$5 + 7 =$ ☐ $4 \times 5 =$ ☐ $16 - 7 =$ ☐

$6 - 4 =$ ☐ $5 + 0 =$ ☐ $3 + 8 =$ ☐

$2 \times 2 =$ ☐ $9 - 8 =$ ☐ $8 \times 8 =$ ☐

$4 - 3 =$ ☐ $12 - 5 =$ ☐ $7 \times 8 =$ ☐

$6 + 9 =$ ☐ $8 + 3 =$ ☐ $15 - 9 =$ ☐

$6 \times 5 =$ ☐ $4 \times 3 =$ ☐ $8 + 4 =$ ☐

$15 - 8 =$ ☐ $8 - 8 =$ ☐ $16 - 8 =$ ☐

$2 + 2 =$ ☐ $2 + 4 =$ ☐ $3 + 2 =$ ☐

$10 - 9 =$ ☐ $4 \times 6 =$ ☐ $8 \times 2 =$ ☐

$6 \times 3 =$ ☐ $11 - 5 =$ ☐ $5 \times 4 =$ ☐

$9 + 5 =$ ☐ $8 - 6 =$ ☐ $6 + 9 =$ ☐

$1 \times 8 =$ ☐ $0 + 8 =$ ☐ $6 - 1 =$ ☐

$14 - 6 =$ ☐ $11 - 8 =$ ☐ $4 + 5 =$ ☐

$2 \times 4 =$ ☐ $6 + 6 =$ ☐ $9 \times 7 =$ ☐

$7 + 5 =$ ☐ $9 \times 4 =$ ☐ $12 - 3 =$ ☐

$3 \times 6 =$ ☐ $9 + 7 =$ ☐

End Time ☐ : ☐

Day 28

Start Time ☐ : ☐

$3 - 1 =$ ☐

$6 \times 2 =$ ☐

$4 + 7 =$ ☐

$6 - 5 =$ ☐

$3 \times 3 =$ ☐

$11 - 5 =$ ☐

$7 + 4 =$ ☐

$2 \times 3 =$ ☐

$5 + 3 =$ ☐

$9 + 5 =$ ☐

$8 \times 8 =$ ☐

$16 - 9 =$ ☐

$9 \times 8 =$ ☐

$7 + 7 =$ ☐

$6 - 6 =$ ☐

$8 \times 7 =$ ☐

$7 \times 2 =$ ☐

$10 - 3 =$ ☐

$2 + 8 =$ ☐

$9 \times 2 =$ ☐

$2 \times 7 =$ ☐

$8 + 0 =$ ☐

$10 - 1 =$ ☐

$8 \times 2 =$ ☐

$9 - 9 =$ ☐

$2 + 3 =$ ☐

$5 + 9 =$ ☐

$9 \times 4 =$ ☐

$11 - 2 =$ ☐

$2 + 6 =$ ☐

$6 - 4 =$ ☐

$3 \times 1 =$ ☐

$7 + 9 =$ ☐

$15 - 7 =$ ☐

$9 + 1 =$ ☐

$9 - 4 =$ ☐

$16 - 7 =$ ☐

$6 + 1 =$ ☐

$3 \times 7 =$ ☐

$7 + 3 =$ ☐

$9 - 7 =$ ☐

$9 \times 7 =$ ☐

$11 - 4 =$ ☐

$9 \times 5 =$ ☐

$7 + 6 =$ ☐

$3 \times 2 =$ ☐

$4 + 2 =$ ☐

$17 - 8 =$ ☐

$2 + 5 =$ ☐

$13 - 7 =$ ☐

Time Required [ ] : [ ]

$16 - 8 =$ [ ]

$7 \times 3 =$ [ ]

$3 + 8 =$ [ ]

$4 + 3 =$ [ ]

$4 \times 6 =$ [ ]

$6 + 8 =$ [ ]

$10 - 2 =$ [ ]

$5 - 5 =$ [ ]

$5 + 9 =$ [ ]

$8 \times 7 =$ [ ]

$11 - 3 =$ [ ]

$5 \times 2 =$ [ ]

$5 \times 7 =$ [ ]

$5 + 5 =$ [ ]

$10 - 8 =$ [ ]

$2 \times 9 =$ [ ]

$7 - 6 =$ [ ]

$6 \times 6 =$ [ ]

$11 - 6 =$ [ ]

$8 - 4 =$ [ ]

$8 + 9 =$ [ ]

$5 \times 6 =$ [ ]

$2 + 7 =$ [ ]

$9 - 5 =$ [ ]

$4 \times 3 =$ [ ]

$15 - 6 =$ [ ]

$4 \times 8 =$ [ ]

$9 + 4 =$ [ ]

$7 \times 7 =$ [ ]

$2 + 0 =$ [ ]

$8 + 7 =$ [ ]

$14 - 8 =$ [ ]

$7 \times 1 =$ [ ]

$13 - 8 =$ [ ]

$6 + 2 =$ [ ]

$4 + 8 =$ [ ]

$6 \times 4 =$ [ ]

$9 - 6 =$ [ ]

$6 + 5 =$ [ ]

$7 \times 6 =$ [ ]

$8 + 6 =$ [ ]

$14 - 6 =$ [ ]

$4 + 1 =$ [ ]

$8 \times 9 =$ [ ]

$5 \times 4 =$ [ ]

$10 - 7 =$ [ ]

$6 + 6 =$ [ ]

$8 + 1 =$ [ ]

$8 \times 6 =$ [ ]

$12 - 3 =$ [ ]

End Time [ ] : [ ]

Day 29

Start Time ☐ : ☐

$9 \times 5 =$ ☐

$6 + 2 =$ ☐

$13 - 7 =$ ☐

$9 + 1 =$ ☐

$7 \times 4 =$ ☐

$9 - 6 =$ ☐

$11 - 8 =$ ☐

$4 + 2 =$ ☐

$10 - 1 =$ ☐

$2 \times 4 =$ ☐

$2 \times 3 =$ ☐

$5 - 0 =$ ☐

$11 - 4 =$ ☐

$7 \times 3 =$ ☐

$2 + 6 =$ ☐

$7 + 7 =$ ☐

$9 \times 7 =$ ☐

$9 + 2 =$ ☐

$4 + 3 =$ ☐

$2 \times 6 =$ ☐

$7 + 9 =$ ☐

$6 \times 1 =$ ☐

$8 - 6 =$ ☐

$11 - 3 =$ ☐

$8 \times 5 =$ ☐

$15 - 6 =$ ☐

$7 + 3 =$ ☐

$6 \times 8 =$ ☐

$2 + 9 =$ ☐

$5 + 0 =$ ☐

$9 \times 4 =$ ☐

$3 + 9 =$ ☐

$9 - 8 =$ ☐

$5 + 7 =$ ☐

$11 - 5 =$ ☐

$9 + 7 =$ ☐

$3 - 1 =$ ☐

$2 \times 9 =$ ☐

$10 - 2 =$ ☐

$1 + 2 =$ ☐

$3 + 7 =$ ☐

$7 - 6 =$ ☐

$3 \times 4 =$ ☐

$14 - 6 =$ ☐

$9 \times 8 =$ ☐

$6 + 6 =$ ☐

$7 - 3 =$ ☐

$3 + 6 =$ ☐

$13 - 8 =$ ☐

$5 \times 5 =$ ☐

$12 - 3 =$ ☐ $8 - 3 =$ ☐ $6 \times 6 =$ ☐

$5 \times 1 =$ ☐ $1 + 5 =$ ☐ $9 + 6 =$ ☐

$9 + 8 =$ ☐ $5 \times 3 =$ ☐ $10 - 4 =$ ☐

$8 - 1 =$ ☐ $10 - 3 =$ ☐ $9 \times 2 =$ ☐

$4 \times 6 =$ ☐ $9 \times 1 =$ ☐ $15 - 8 =$ ☐

$16 - 9 =$ ☐ $1 + 2 =$ ☐ $7 + 8 =$ ☐

$6 - 5 =$ ☐ $5 \times 4 =$ ☐ $3 + 4 =$ ☐

$6 + 4 =$ ☐ $2 + 8 =$ ☐ $8 - 6 =$ ☐

$5 \times 8 =$ ☐ $13 - 4 =$ ☐ $6 \times 9 =$ ☐

$14 - 7 =$ ☐ $3 \times 8 =$ ☐ $4 + 7 =$ ☐

$7 \times 2 =$ ☐ $4 + 5 =$ ☐ $3 - 3 =$ ☐

$5 + 3 =$ ☐ $8 + 6 =$ ☐ $7 \times 8 =$ ☐

$8 + 7 =$ ☐ $14 - 5 =$ ☐ $0 + 8 =$ ☐

$6 \times 2 =$ ☐ $3 \times 6 =$ ☐ $10 - 6 =$ ☐

$11 - 9 =$ ☐ $11 - 7 =$ ☐ $9 + 4 =$ ☐

$7 + 5 =$ ☐ $7 \times 9 =$ ☐ $7 - 2 =$ ☐

$6 \times 3 =$ ☐ $6 + 7 =$ ☐

End Time ☐ : ☐

Date ☐ M ☐ D

Start Time ☐ : ☐

$1 + 4 =$ ☐

$9 \times 3 =$ ☐

$11 - 3 =$ ☐

$5 + 9 =$ ☐

$1 - 1 =$ ☐

$9 \times 1 =$ ☐

$3 + 1 =$ ☐

$15 - 7 =$ ☐

$7 \times 7 =$ ☐

$12 - 5 =$ ☐

$8 + 2 =$ ☐

$8 - 4 =$ ☐

$9 + 5 =$ ☐

$5 + 0 =$ ☐

$8 \times 6 =$ ☐

$16 - 8 =$ ☐

$5 + 6 =$ ☐

$6 - 3 =$ ☐

$6 + 2 =$ ☐

$6 + 7 =$ ☐

$5 \times 5 =$ ☐

$7 - 3 =$ ☐

$7 \times 6 =$ ☐

$14 - 5 =$ ☐

$4 + 8 =$ ☐

$8 \times 3 =$ ☐

$1 + 8 =$ ☐

$14 - 6 =$ ☐

$9 - 9 =$ ☐

$8 \times 8 =$ ☐

$8 + 7 =$ ☐

$17 - 9 =$ ☐

$3 \times 7 =$ ☐

$13 - 5 =$ ☐

$9 \times 7 =$ ☐

$8 + 5 =$ ☐

$7 \times 8 =$ ☐

$1 \times 6 =$ ☐

$3 + 9 =$ ☐

$8 - 1 =$ ☐

$4 \times 2 =$ ☐

$11 - 5 =$ ☐

$3 + 6 =$ ☐

$5 + 9 =$ ☐

$14 - 9 =$ ☐

$5 \times 7 =$ ☐

$7 - 6 =$ ☐

$8 \times 7 =$ ☐

$4 \times 7 =$ ☐

$2 + 4 =$ ☐

$18 - 9 =$ ☐ $8 + 6 =$ ☐ $2 \times 4 =$ ☐

$6 + 5 =$ ☐ $13 - 4 =$ ☐ $4 + 1 =$ ☐

$2 \times 9 =$ ☐ $0 \times 7 =$ ☐ $12 - 4 =$ ☐

$14 - 8 =$ ☐ $8 - 2 =$ ☐ $7 + 9 =$ ☐

$3 \times 6 =$ ☐ $3 \times 9 =$ ☐ $5 \times 1 =$ ☐

$3 + 7 =$ ☐ $6 + 6 =$ ☐ $5 \times 3 =$ ☐

$9 - 5 =$ ☐ $10 - 2 =$ ☐ $3 + 5 =$ ☐

$1 + 6 =$ ☐ $1 + 9 =$ ☐ $10 - 8 =$ ☐

$15 - 6 =$ ☐ $9 \times 8 =$ ☐ $9 + 4 =$ ☐

$2 + 7 =$ ☐ $7 - 2 =$ ☐ $6 \times 7 =$ ☐

$10 - 3 =$ ☐ $6 \times 6 =$ ☐ $6 \times 8 =$ ☐

$9 + 8 =$ ☐ $6 - 0 =$ ☐ $12 - 3 =$ ☐

$9 - 3 =$ ☐ $4 + 7 =$ ☐ $1 + 7 =$ ☐

$6 \times 5 =$ ☐ $7 \times 5 =$ ☐ $9 \times 9 =$ ☐

$7 + 8 =$ ☐ $4 \times 4 =$ ☐ $11 - 7 =$ ☐

$8 \times 5 =$ ☐ $5 + 3 =$ ☐ $8 + 8 =$ ☐

$5 - 4 =$ ☐ $10 - 7 =$ ☐

I. Counting Test

Measure the time required for you to count from 1 to 120 aloud as fast as you can.

☐ sec.

II. Word Memorization Test

Memorize as many words as you can **within two minutes**.

everyone	film	salt	mark	text	paddle
tree	hair	season	beat	letter	fountain
west	idea	game	size	front	bone
tractor	place	meat	niece	order	string
question	arrow	fork	cloth	stove	wonder

Write out as many words as you can remember **in two minutes** on the back of this page. How many words can you remember?

Number of words memorized ☐ words

Week 6

Word Memorization Test Answers

III. Stroop Test

Please take the **Stroop Test** for Week 6, located on page **ix** of the Appendix.

Date ☐ M ☐ D

Start Time ☐ : ☐

$3 + 3 =$ ☐

$8 \times 6 =$ ☐

$5 - 4 =$ ☐

$2 \times 5 =$ ☐

$7 + 9 =$ ☐

$14 - 6 =$ ☐

$5 + 2 =$ ☐

$3 \times 2 =$ ☐

$0 \times 3 =$ ☐

$8 - 5 =$ ☐

$9 + 2 =$ ☐

$9 - 3 =$ ☐

$4 + 8 =$ ☐

$17 - 9 =$ ☐

$8 + 2 =$ ☐

$4 \times 5 =$ ☐

$16 - 7 =$ ☐

$2 \times 9 =$ ☐

$14 - 5 =$ ☐

$3 + 8 =$ ☐

$8 + 9 =$ ☐

$6 \times 8 =$ ☐

$6 + 2 =$ ☐

$9 \times 7 =$ ☐

$6 - 3 =$ ☐

$8 + 8 =$ ☐

$10 - 9 =$ ☐

$5 + 7 =$ ☐

$5 \times 6 =$ ☐

$8 - 6 =$ ☐

$3 + 4 =$ ☐

$9 \times 5 =$ ☐

$15 - 6 =$ ☐

$6 \times 7 =$ ☐

$2 + 4 =$ ☐

$1 \times 4 =$ ☐

$4 \times 9 =$ ☐

$9 - 6 =$ ☐

$4 + 5 =$ ☐

$7 + 5 =$ ☐

$12 - 3 =$ ☐

$6 \times 2 =$ ☐

$11 - 2 =$ ☐

$7 - 2 =$ ☐

$8 \times 8 =$ ☐

$3 + 1 =$ ☐

$11 - 3 =$ ☐

$9 + 6 =$ ☐

$12 - 7 =$ ☐

$8 \times 9 =$ ☐

$3 + 5 =$ [   ] $5 \times 1 =$ [   ] $13 - 6 =$ [   ]

$8 + 6 =$ [   ] $3 \times 6 =$ [   ] $8 + 1 =$ [   ]

$4 - 2 =$ [   ] $3 + 7 =$ [   ] $2 - 1 =$ [   ]

$9 \times 8 =$ [   ] $11 - 4 =$ [   ] $5 \times 5 =$ [   ]

$9 + 1 =$ [   ] $4 \times 0 =$ [   ] $7 - 7 =$ [   ]

$1 \times 4 =$ [   ] $6 + 3 =$ [   ] $11 - 8 =$ [   ]

$12 - 5 =$ [   ] $5 + 8 =$ [   ] $4 + 8 =$ [   ]

$7 - 5 =$ [   ] $10 - 5 =$ [   ] $9 \times 9 =$ [   ]

$4 + 9 =$ [   ] $7 \times 3 =$ [   ] $4 + 4 =$ [   ]

$2 \times 7 =$ [   ] $9 \times 2 =$ [   ] $8 + 5 =$ [   ]

$15 - 8 =$ [   ] $7 + 1 =$ [   ] $4 \times 7 =$ [   ]

$5 + 1 =$ [   ] $7 + 6 =$ [   ] $10 - 1 =$ [   ]

$8 - 6 =$ [   ] $9 - 5 =$ [   ] $5 \times 7 =$ [   ]

$10 - 3 =$ [   ] $2 \times 3 =$ [   ] $15 - 9 =$ [   ]

$9 + 8 =$ [   ] $5 \times 3 =$ [   ] $3 + 9 =$ [   ]

$5 \times 4 =$ [   ] $14 - 9 =$ [   ] $7 \times 2 =$ [   ]

$16 - 9 =$ [   ] $9 + 4 =$ [   ]

End Time [   ] : [   ]

Date ☐ M ☐ D

Start Time ☐ : ☐

$2 + 6 =$ ☐

$10 - 2 =$ ☐

$3 - 3 =$ ☐

$11 - 5 =$ ☐

$5 + 3 =$ ☐

$3 + 1 =$ ☐

$6 + 7 =$ ☐

$3 \times 3 =$ ☐

$9 \times 7 =$ ☐

$9 \times 9 =$ ☐

$9 + 4 =$ ☐

$8 + 2 =$ ☐

$3 - 1 =$ ☐

$5 - 4 =$ ☐

$4 \times 7 =$ ☐

$8 \times 7 =$ ☐

$6 \times 9 =$ ☐

$8 - 7 =$ ☐

$9 + 0 =$ ☐

$1 - 0 =$ ☐

$7 + 4 =$ ☐

$9 \times 3 =$ ☐

$5 + 4 =$ ☐

$13 - 7 =$ ☐

$4 \times 3 =$ ☐

$14 - 7 =$ ☐

$2 + 3 =$ ☐

$9 - 3 =$ ☐

$3 \times 6 =$ ☐

$8 \times 6 =$ ☐

$4 + 9 =$ ☐

$7 + 6 =$ ☐

$17 - 9 =$ ☐

$2 \times 8 =$ ☐

$12 - 3 =$ ☐

$7 + 7 =$ ☐

$14 - 8 =$ ☐

$16 - 9 =$ ☐

$5 \times 7 =$ ☐

$3 \times 4 =$ ☐

$2 \times 7 =$ ☐

$7 - 1 =$ ☐

$14 - 6 =$ ☐

$6 + 8 =$ ☐

$11 - 8 =$ ☐

$2 \times 6 =$ ☐

$13 - 6 =$ ☐

$1 \times 6 =$ ☐

$9 + 8 =$ ☐

$7 + 3 =$ ☐

$3 \times 2 =$ [ ] $3 + 2 =$ [ ] $4 \times 9 =$ [ ]

$7 - 4 =$ [ ] $8 \times 3 =$ [ ] $4 - 3 =$ [ ]

$4 + 1 =$ [ ] $9 - 5 =$ [ ] $12 - 4 =$ [ ]

$15 - 8 =$ [ ] $8 + 8 =$ [ ] $5 + 2 =$ [ ]

$8 + 9 =$ [ ] $5 \times 3 =$ [ ] $2 + 8 =$ [ ]

$8 \times 5 =$ [ ] $4 + 0 =$ [ ] $3 \times 7 =$ [ ]

$8 \times 4 =$ [ ] $13 - 8 =$ [ ] $5 - 5 =$ [ ]

$8 + 1 =$ [ ] $6 \times 2 =$ [ ] $7 + 1 =$ [ ]

$6 \times 4 =$ [ ] $9 + 9 =$ [ ] $5 \times 9 =$ [ ]

$8 - 8 =$ [ ] $5 - 1 =$ [ ] $9 + 6 =$ [ ]

$6 \times 0 =$ [ ] $1 \times 8 =$ [ ] $10 - 5 =$ [ ]

$3 + 7 =$ [ ] $16 - 8 =$ [ ] $4 + 7 =$ [ ]

$10 - 8 =$ [ ] $3 + 9 =$ [ ] $10 - 6 =$ [ ]

$7 \times 9 =$ [ ] $4 \times 4 =$ [ ] $9 \times 2 =$ [ ]

$16 - 7 =$ [ ] $11 - 4 =$ [ ] $8 + 6 =$ [ ]

$7 + 8 =$ [ ] $9 + 1 =$ [ ] $11 - 9 =$ [ ]

$11 - 7 =$ [ ] $2 \times 3 =$ [ ]

End Time [ ] : [ ]

Start Time ☐ : ☐

$4 + 0 =$ ☐

$7 - 4 =$ ☐

$5 \times 3 =$ ☐

$10 - 4 =$ ☐

$5 + 2 =$ ☐

$3 \times 4 =$ ☐

$8 - 7 =$ ☐

$5 \times 5 =$ ☐

$17 - 9 =$ ☐

$0 \times 7 =$ ☐

$8 + 8 =$ ☐

$4 \times 2 =$ ☐

$2 \times 9 =$ ☐

$9 + 7 =$ ☐

$15 - 6 =$ ☐

$8 + 3 =$ ☐

$9 \times 2 =$ ☐

$14 - 7 =$ ☐

$2 + 7 =$ ☐

$7 \times 9 =$ ☐

$13 - 8 =$ ☐

$5 \times 1 =$ ☐

$7 + 4 =$ ☐

$9 - 4 =$ ☐

$3 + 2 =$ ☐

$8 - 3 =$ ☐

$7 \times 4 =$ ☐

$6 + 7 =$ ☐

$7 - 3 =$ ☐

$9 + 3 =$ ☐

$7 \times 7 =$ ☐

$2 + 9 =$ ☐

$12 - 3 =$ ☐

$2 + 5 =$ ☐

$6 \times 3 =$ ☐

$8 - 1 =$ ☐

$6 + 8 =$ ☐

$6 \times 7 =$ ☐

$1 + 8 =$ ☐

$8 \times 6 =$ ☐

$5 + 3 =$ ☐

$10 - 6 =$ ☐

$4 - 0 =$ ☐

$7 + 5 =$ ☐

$8 \times 8 =$ ☐

$10 - 1 =$ ☐

$10 - 8 =$ ☐

$2 \times 2 =$ ☐

$13 - 7 =$ ☐

$9 + 2 =$ ☐

$9 - 3 =$ [ ]

$16 - 7 =$ [ ]

$3 + 5 =$ [ ]

$8 \times 1 =$ [ ]

$14 - 9 =$ [ ]

$2 \times 8 =$ [ ]

$7 + 2 =$ [ ]

$11 - 6 =$ [ ]

$4 - 4 =$ [ ]

$5 \times 7 =$ [ ]

$11 - 4 =$ [ ]

$8 + 6 =$ [ ]

$7 \times 6 =$ [ ]

$9 + 9 =$ [ ]

$18 - 9 =$ [ ]

$2 + 8 =$ [ ]

$0 \times 9 =$ [ ]

$0 + 6 =$ [ ]

$8 - 4 =$ [ ]

$3 \times 9 =$ [ ]

$6 \times 4 =$ [ ]

$3 + 9 =$ [ ]

$5 \times 8 =$ [ ]

$11 - 9 =$ [ ]

$7 + 1 =$ [ ]

$4 \times 8 =$ [ ]

$7 + 9 =$ [ ]

$9 - 1 =$ [ ]

$8 \times 4 =$ [ ]

$12 - 7 =$ [ ]

$3 + 3 =$ [ ]

$13 - 9 =$ [ ]

$3 \times 3 =$ [ ]

$4 + 7 =$ [ ]

$9 \times 4 =$ [ ]

$2 - 1 =$ [ ]

$6 + 3 =$ [ ]

$11 - 2 =$ [ ]

$9 \times 8 =$ [ ]

$5 + 5 =$ [ ]

$6 \times 6 =$ [ ]

$5 + 9 =$ [ ]

$8 \times 2 =$ [ ]

$4 + 9 =$ [ ]

$9 - 7 =$ [ ]

$12 - 8 =$ [ ]

$3 + 8 =$ [ ]

$2 \times 5 =$ [ ]

$5 + 8 =$ [ ]

$10 - 2 =$ [ ]

End Time [ ] : [ ]

Start Time [ ] : [ ]

$2 \times 5 =$ [ ]

$9 - 1 =$ [ ]

$4 + 2 =$ [ ]

$3 \times 2 =$ [ ]

$2 + 9 =$ [ ]

$7 - 4 =$ [ ]

$12 - 3 =$ [ ]

$7 \times 8 =$ [ ]

$10 - 4 =$ [ ]

$8 + 4 =$ [ ]

$5 + 5 =$ [ ]

$9 \times 6 =$ [ ]

$3 + 3 =$ [ ]

$5 \times 6 =$ [ ]

$0 \times 7 =$ [ ]

$8 + 5 =$ [ ]

$8 \times 2 =$ [ ]

$6 - 5 =$ [ ]

$1 + 0 =$ [ ]

$5 - 3 =$ [ ]

$7 \times 7 =$ [ ]

$15 - 7 =$ [ ]

$3 + 4 =$ [ ]

$8 + 9 =$ [ ]

$9 - 8 =$ [ ]

$3 \times 1 =$ [ ]

$13 - 6 =$ [ ]

$6 \times 6 =$ [ ]

$3 + 7 =$ [ ]

$10 - 9 =$ [ ]

$9 + 5 =$ [ ]

$15 - 9 =$ [ ]

$4 \times 3 =$ [ ]

$8 - 5 =$ [ ]

$4 + 1 =$ [ ]

$1 \times 9 =$ [ ]

$11 - 6 =$ [ ]

$9 + 3 =$ [ ]

$5 \times 8 =$ [ ]

$4 - 1 =$ [ ]

$9 \times 8 =$ [ ]

$8 + 1 =$ [ ]

$14 - 7 =$ [ ]

$7 + 7 =$ [ ]

$9 \times 2 =$ [ ]

$5 + 3 =$ [ ]

$12 - 6 =$ [ ]

$3 \times 3 =$ [ ]

$5 + 7 =$ [ ]

$10 - 6 =$ [ ]

$5 \times 6 =$ ☐ $3 + 5 =$ ☐ $3 - 1 =$ ☐

$8 - 1 =$ ☐ $9 + 8 =$ ☐ $1 \times 5 =$ ☐

$6 + 8 =$ ☐ $7 \times 4 =$ ☐ $6 + 7 =$ ☐

$11 - 9 =$ ☐ $4 - 3 =$ ☐ $4 + 0 =$ ☐

$8 \times 4 =$ ☐ $8 + 8 =$ ☐ $8 \times 9 =$ ☐

$2 + 2 =$ ☐ $2 \times 9 =$ ☐ $4 + 6 =$ ☐

$9 - 4 =$ ☐ $5 + 6 =$ ☐ $15 - 8 =$ ☐

$7 \times 1 =$ ☐ $14 - 8 =$ ☐ $8 - 3 =$ ☐

$13 - 8 =$ ☐ $7 + 1 =$ ☐ $1 + 1 =$ ☐

$4 \times 7 =$ ☐ $11 - 3 =$ ☐ $6 \times 8 =$ ☐

$7 + 3 =$ ☐ $8 \times 8 =$ ☐ $10 - 7 =$ ☐

$6 - 2 =$ ☐ $11 - 7 =$ ☐ $3 \times 8 =$ ☐

$2 + 4 =$ ☐ $5 \times 9 =$ ☐ $2 + 8 =$ ☐

$8 + 6 =$ ☐ $9 + 9 =$ ☐ $6 \times 7 =$ ☐

$11 - 4 =$ ☐ $4 + 9 =$ ☐ $12 - 5 =$ ☐

$9 \times 9 =$ ☐ $10 - 2 =$ ☐ $4 \times 8 =$ ☐

$15 - 6 =$ ☐ $4 \times 9 =$ ☐

End Time ☐ : ☐

Start Time ☐ : ☐

$10 - 6 =$ ☐

$5 + 0 =$ ☐

$7 \times 7 =$ ☐

$8 - 7 =$ ☐

$4 + 4 =$ ☐

$13 - 5 =$ ☐

$7 \times 3 =$ ☐

$3 \times 8 =$ ☐

$5 + 4 =$ ☐

$9 + 5 =$ ☐

$5 \times 7 =$ ☐

$13 - 9 =$ ☐

$3 + 8 =$ ☐

$9 - 2 =$ ☐

$9 \times 8 =$ ☐

$4 + 7 =$ ☐

$2 \times 5 =$ ☐

$9 + 9 =$ ☐

$5 - 3 =$ ☐

$18 - 9 =$ ☐

$7 + 2 =$ ☐

$5 \times 9 =$ ☐

$7 + 6 =$ ☐

$9 - 7 =$ ☐

$4 \times 6 =$ ☐

$11 - 2 =$ ☐

$4 \times 9 =$ ☐

$2 + 8 =$ ☐

$7 \times 0 =$ ☐

$2 + 5 =$ ☐

$10 - 5 =$ ☐

$8 + 7 =$ ☐

$6 \times 5 =$ ☐

$13 - 7 =$ ☐

$9 - 9 =$ ☐

$6 + 1 =$ ☐

$3 + 7 =$ ☐

$6 - 3 =$ ☐

$8 \times 5 =$ ☐

$15 - 8 =$ ☐

$4 + 6 =$ ☐

$8 \times 9 =$ ☐

$3 + 4 =$ ☐

$7 - 5 =$ ☐

$2 \times 3 =$ ☐

$10 - 9 =$ ☐

$7 \times 6 =$ ☐

$7 + 7 =$ ☐

$9 \times 7 =$ ☐

$13 - 8 =$ ☐

$8 - 4 =$ [ ]

$0 + 3 =$ [ ]

$7 \times 4 =$ [ ]

$15 - 6 =$ [ ]

$4 \times 4 =$ [ ]

$9 - 4 =$ [ ]

$8 \times 7 =$ [ ]

$6 + 6 =$ [ ]

$14 - 9 =$ [ ]

$9 \times 6 =$ [ ]

$1 + 7 =$ [ ]

$7 + 9 =$ [ ]

$11 - 5 =$ [ ]

$5 \times 2 =$ [ ]

$12 - 9 =$ [ ]

$2 \times 2 =$ [ ]

$7 + 5 =$ [ ]

$6 \times 7 =$ [ ]

$7 + 3 =$ [ ]

$14 - 5 =$ [ ]

$6 \times 9 =$ [ ]

$14 - 7 =$ [ ]

$8 + 4 =$ [ ]

$2 + 6 =$ [ ]

$9 - 5 =$ [ ]

$2 \times 4 =$ [ ]

$4 + 8 =$ [ ]

$4 - 3 =$ [ ]

$7 \times 2 =$ [ ]

$5 + 3 =$ [ ]

$15 - 7 =$ [ ]

$8 + 6 =$ [ ]

$12 - 9 =$ [ ]

$8 \times 1 =$ [ ]

$16 - 8 =$ [ ]

$5 \times 5 =$ [ ]

$9 + 1 =$ [ ]

$2 + 3 =$ [ ]

$9 \times 2 =$ [ ]

$4 - 4 =$ [ ]

$6 + 2 =$ [ ]

$3 - 1 =$ [ ]

$4 \times 2 =$ [ ]

$17 - 9 =$ [ ]

$8 + 9 =$ [ ]

$3 \times 5 =$ [ ]

$5 + 8 =$ [ ]

$7 \times 8 =$ [ ]

$10 - 1 =$ [ ]

$7 + 4 =$ [ ]

End Time [ ] : [ ]

I. Counting Test

Measure the time required for you to count from 1 to 120 aloud as fast as you can.

☐ sec.

II. Word Memorization Test

Memorize as many words as you can **within two minutes.**

camp	notice	answer	eagle	liquid	village
mean	crop	bill	person	target	center
fall	hand	race	unit	shuttle	dairy
image	night	foil	mother	war	butter
plan	trade	straw	row	duty	soil

Write out as many words as you can remember **in two minutes** on the back of this page. How many words can you remember?

Number of words memorized ☐ words

Word Memorization Test Answers

III. Stroop Test

Please take the **Stroop Test** for Week 7, located on page **x** of the Appendix.

Date ☐ M ☐ D

Start Time ☐ : ☐

$4 \times 9 =$ ☐

$13 - 4 =$ ☐

$7 + 8 =$ ☐

$6 + 6 =$ ☐

$5 \times 9 =$ ☐

$3 + 2 =$ ☐

$1 \times 5 =$ ☐

$7 - 2 =$ ☐

$8 + 8 =$ ☐

$16 - 7 =$ ☐

$9 + 3 =$ ☐

$4 \times 3 =$ ☐

$9 - 5 =$ ☐

$2 + 7 =$ ☐

$9 \times 3 =$ ☐

$10 - 9 =$ ☐

$8 \times 2 =$ ☐

$4 + 0 =$ ☐

$6 \times 4 =$ ☐

$1 \times 3 =$ ☐

$8 - 6 =$ ☐

$5 + 3 =$ ☐

$5 + 9 =$ ☐

$14 - 6 =$ ☐

$5 \times 5 =$ ☐

$10 - 6 =$ ☐

$7 - 3 =$ ☐

$7 \times 6 =$ ☐

$1 + 5 =$ ☐

$13 - 8 =$ ☐

$7 + 6 =$ ☐

$12 - 8 =$ ☐

$9 \times 8 =$ ☐

$13 - 5 =$ ☐

$1 + 7 =$ ☐

$2 \times 3 =$ ☐

$9 - 4 =$ ☐

$4 \times 2 =$ ☐

$6 + 5 =$ ☐

$12 - 4 =$ ☐

$4 + 1 =$ ☐

$3 \times 4 =$ ☐

$5 \times 3 =$ ☐

$6 - 2 =$ ☐

$4 + 6 =$ ☐

$5 - 2 =$ ☐

$8 + 5 =$ ☐

$11 - 2 =$ ☐

$4 + 9 =$ ☐

$6 \times 8 =$ ☐

$9 \times 2 =$ [ ]

$7 \times 5 =$ [ ]

$9 + 2 =$ [ ]

$17 - 9 =$ [ ]

$8 \times 0 =$ [ ]

$4 + 3 =$ [ ]

$5 + 8 =$ [ ]

$12 - 5 =$ [ ]

$9 \times 5 =$ [ ]

$2 \times 7 =$ [ ]

$1 + 8 =$ [ ]

$3 + 7 =$ [ ]

$8 - 5 =$ [ ]

$3 \times 3 =$ [ ]

$3 \times 9 =$ [ ]

$12 - 7 =$ [ ]

$6 + 4 =$ [ ]

$15 - 6 =$ [ ]

$8 + 1 =$ [ ]

$2 - 2 =$ [ ]

$3 \times 2 =$ [ ]

$6 - 2 =$ [ ]

$10 - 1 =$ [ ]

$9 + 6 =$ [ ]

$5 \times 6 =$ [ ]

$5 + 1 =$ [ ]

$8 + 6 =$ [ ]

$6 \times 3 =$ [ ]

$13 - 6 =$ [ ]

$3 \times 7 =$ [ ]

$14 - 9 =$ [ ]

$1 + 9 =$ [ ]

$7 \times 1 =$ [ ]

$18 - 9 =$ [ ]

$4 + 2 =$ [ ]

$8 + 9 =$ [ ]

$5 - 4 =$ [ ]

$7 \times 8 =$ [ ]

$6 + 7 =$ [ ]

$9 \times 6 =$ [ ]

$15 - 7 =$ [ ]

$9 - 8 =$ [ ]

$9 + 9 =$ [ ]

$6 \times 7 =$ [ ]

$10 - 2 =$ [ ]

$1 + 6 =$ [ ]

$4 - 3 =$ [ ]

$16 - 9 =$ [ ]

$6 + 8 =$ [ ]

$4 \times 8 =$ [ ]

End Time [ ] : [ ]

Start Time [ ] : [ ]

$11 - 2 =$ [ ]

$9 + 4 =$ [ ]

$1 \times 8 =$ [ ]

$9 - 6 =$ [ ]

$2 \times 2 =$ [ ]

$4 + 5 =$ [ ]

$2 \times 4 =$ [ ]

$8 \times 5 =$ [ ]

$7 - 1 =$ [ ]

$7 + 5 =$ [ ]

$5 \times 4 =$ [ ]

$11 - 4 =$ [ ]

$3 \times 2 =$ [ ]

$14 - 7 =$ [ ]

$3 \times 4 =$ [ ]

$6 + 9 =$ [ ]

$14 - 9 =$ [ ]

$2 + 4 =$ [ ]

$7 \times 7 =$ [ ]

$3 + 8 =$ [ ]

$6 - 4 =$ [ ]

$3 \times 5 =$ [ ]

$4 - 4 =$ [ ]

$8 + 0 =$ [ ]

$17 - 8 =$ [ ]

$6 \times 4 =$ [ ]

$5 + 5 =$ [ ]

$4 + 9 =$ [ ]

$13 - 6 =$ [ ]

$2 \times 9 =$ [ ]

$5 + 7 =$ [ ]

$13 - 9 =$ [ ]

$1 + 9 =$ [ ]

$7 + 0 =$ [ ]

$7 - 5 =$ [ ]

$6 + 3 =$ [ ]

$4 \times 2 =$ [ ]

$7 + 3 =$ [ ]

$9 \times 9 =$ [ ]

$9 - 2 =$ [ ]

$6 + 7 =$ [ ]

$12 - 8 =$ [ ]

$1 + 2 =$ [ ]

$7 \times 9 =$ [ ]

$12 - 4 =$ [ ]

$9 + 9 =$ [ ]

$8 \times 4 =$ [ ]

$9 \times 2 =$ [ ]

$15 - 9 =$ [ ]

$9 \times 8 =$ [ ]

$1 + 3 =$ [ ]

$7 \times 4 =$ [ ]

$9 - 8 =$ [ ]

$6 + 8 =$ [ ]

$9 \times 6 =$ [ ]

$2 + 2 =$ [ ]

$10 - 3 =$ [ ]

$4 \times 5 =$ [ ]

$8 + 9 =$ [ ]

$8 - 3 =$ [ ]

$6 \times 5 =$ [ ]

$14 - 8 =$ [ ]

$5 + 9 =$ [ ]

$7 \times 3 =$ [ ]

$12 - 9 =$ [ ]

$7 + 8 =$ [ ]

$6 \times 0 =$ [ ]

$8 \times 8 =$ [ ]

$6 - 2 =$ [ ]

$15 - 7 =$ [ ]

$4 + 1 =$ [ ]

$8 + 3 =$ [ ]

$4 \times 7 =$ [ ]

$9 - 7 =$ [ ]

$1 + 5 =$ [ ]

$2 \times 3 =$ [ ]

$8 + 4 =$ [ ]

$18 - 9 =$ [ ]

$6 \times 7 =$ [ ]

$10 - 2 =$ [ ]

$8 \times 6 =$ [ ]

$9 + 8 =$ [ ]

$10 - 6 =$ [ ]

$13 - 7 =$ [ ]

$2 \times 6 =$ [ ]

$5 - 0 =$ [ ]

$3 + 2 =$ [ ]

$10 - 4 =$ [ ]

$2 + 9 =$ [ ]

$5 \times 3 =$ [ ]

$8 \times 9 =$ [ ]

$4 + 3 =$ [ ]

$6 \times 8 =$ [ ]

$8 - 7 =$ [ ]

$4 \times 3 =$ [ ]

$7 + 7 =$ [ ]

$11 - 3 =$ [ ]

$3 \times 7 =$ [ ]

$11 - 7 =$ [ ]

$3 + 9 =$ [ ]

End Time [ ] : [ ]

Start Time ☐ : ☐

$14 - 5 =$ ☐

$1 + 0 =$ ☐

$8 \times 9 =$ ☐

$14 - 7 =$ ☐

$9 \times 7 =$ ☐

$5 + 5 =$ ☐

$4 - 1 =$ ☐

$6 + 2 =$ ☐

$6 - 4 =$ ☐

$3 \times 2 =$ ☐

$4 + 8 =$ ☐

$9 - 6 =$ ☐

$8 + 6 =$ ☐

$3 \times 4 =$ ☐

$7 + 5 =$ ☐

$11 - 2 =$ ☐

$3 + 5 =$ ☐

$2 \times 9 =$ ☐

$9 - 8 =$ ☐

$4 + 7 =$ ☐

$9 \times 3 =$ ☐

$5 + 2 =$ ☐

$6 \times 9 =$ ☐

$1 + 1 =$ ☐

$10 - 9 =$ ☐

$5 - 4 =$ ☐

$9 + 5 =$ ☐

$0 \times 7 =$ ☐

$11 - 6 =$ ☐

$10 - 3 =$ ☐

$9 \times 5 =$ ☐

$11 - 3 =$ ☐

$8 + 4 =$ ☐

$6 \times 5 =$ ☐

$8 + 0 =$ ☐

$7 - 3 =$ ☐

$1 \times 9 =$ ☐

$14 - 6 =$ ☐

$5 + 4 =$ ☐

$4 \times 8 =$ ☐

$6 - 3 =$ ☐

$5 \times 2 =$ ☐

$15 - 6 =$ ☐

$2 \times 7 =$ ☐

$9 + 4 =$ ☐

$6 \times 3 =$ ☐

$2 \times 4 =$ ☐

$8 + 2 =$ ☐

$10 - 2 =$ ☐

$5 + 8 =$ ☐

$4 + 3 =$ ☐

$5 - 5 =$ ☐

$9 \times 4 =$ ☐

$5 \times 3 =$ ☐

$4 + 9 =$ ☐

$2 \times 5 =$ ☐

$16 - 8 =$ ☐

$1 + 8 =$ ☐

$3 \times 3 =$ ☐

$7 + 4 =$ ☐

$6 - 2 =$ ☐

$7 \times 5 =$ ☐

$15 - 9 =$ ☐

$2 + 3 =$ ☐

$13 - 5 =$ ☐

$9 \times 8 =$ ☐

$6 + 4 =$ ☐

$7 \times 3 =$ ☐

$4 - 3 =$ ☐

$1 + 6 =$ ☐

$11 - 5 =$ ☐

$2 \times 1 =$ ☐

$9 + 2 =$ ☐

$4 \times 3 =$ ☐

$6 + 9 =$ ☐

$3 \times 8 =$ ☐

$7 + 6 =$ ☐

$3 - 1 =$ ☐

$12 - 5 =$ ☐

$6 + 7 =$ ☐

$5 \times 8 =$ ☐

$2 + 9 =$ ☐

$12 - 7 =$ ☐

$6 \times 4 =$ ☐

$4 - 2 =$ ☐

$17 - 9 =$ ☐

$2 + 5 =$ ☐

$5 \times 4 =$ ☐

$14 - 9 =$ ☐

$4 \times 7 =$ ☐

$7 + 2 =$ ☐

$11 - 4 =$ ☐

$8 - 5 =$ ☐

$2 \times 2 =$ ☐

$18 - 9 =$ ☐

$9 + 1 =$ ☐

$6 \times 6 =$ ☐

$4 + 6 =$ ☐

$12 - 4 =$ ☐

$4 + 9 =$ ☐

End Time ☐ : ☐

Date ☐ M ☐ D

Start Time ☐ : ☐

$8 - 3 =$ ☐

$3 + 2 =$ ☐

$7 - 6 =$ ☐

$3 \times 3 =$ ☐

$10 - 7 =$ ☐

$5 + 2 =$ ☐

$7 + 8 =$ ☐

$5 - 5 =$ ☐

$8 \times 2 =$ ☐

$13 - 4 =$ ☐

$5 \times 4 =$ ☐

$8 + 2 =$ ☐

$16 - 8 =$ ☐

$9 + 1 =$ ☐

$10 - 5 =$ ☐

$9 \times 3 =$ ☐

$8 - 4 =$ ☐

$6 + 0 =$ ☐

$9 \times 5 =$ ☐

$10 - 8 =$ ☐

$1 + 9 =$ ☐

$3 \times 6 =$ ☐

$9 - 5 =$ ☐

$1 \times 4 =$ ☐

$5 + 3 =$ ☐

$18 - 9 =$ ☐

$9 + 8 =$ ☐

$8 \times 3 =$ ☐

$1 + 6 =$ ☐

$10 - 2 =$ ☐

$5 \times 9 =$ ☐

$6 + 5 =$ ☐

$14 - 7 =$ ☐

$5 \times 5 =$ ☐

$4 \times 9 =$ ☐

$9 - 7 =$ ☐

$4 + 4 =$ ☐

$6 \times 5 =$ ☐

$5 + 9 =$ ☐

$7 - 2 =$ ☐

$10 - 4 =$ ☐

$3 \times 9 =$ ☐

$11 - 3 =$ ☐

$3 + 8 =$ ☐

$4 + 6 =$ ☐

$2 \times 3 =$ ☐

$5 + 3 =$ ☐

$3 \times 2 =$ ☐

$8 \times 5 =$ ☐

$3 + 7 =$ ☐

$1 + 3 =$ ☐

$5 + 8 =$ ☐

$9 \times 4 =$ ☐

$4 - 3 =$ ☐

$3 + 9 =$ ☐

$7 \times 5 =$ ☐

$6 + 7 =$ ☐

$9 \times 2 =$ ☐

$5 + 1 =$ ☐

$13 - 5 =$ ☐

$7 \times 9 =$ ☐

$10 - 1 =$ ☐

$6 \times 6 =$ ☐

$2 + 8 =$ ☐

$7 + 4 =$ ☐

$12 - 3 =$ ☐

$4 \times 6 =$ ☐

$9 - 0 =$ ☐

$4 \times 3 =$ ☐

$2 + 9 =$ ☐

$2 + 5 =$ ☐

$9 \times 3 =$ ☐

$8 + 7 =$ ☐

$13 - 7 =$ ☐

$8 - 1 =$ ☐

$4 + 2 =$ ☐

$7 \times 8 =$ ☐

$12 - 9 =$ ☐

$9 \times 9 =$ ☐

$8 + 5 =$ ☐

$2 \times 2 =$ ☐

$10 - 9 =$ ☐

$3 \times 7 =$ ☐

$11 - 4 =$ ☐

$3 \times 8 =$ ☐

$3 - 3 =$ ☐

$6 + 9 =$ ☐

$15 - 7 =$ ☐

$8 \times 7 =$ ☐

$3 + 4 =$ ☐

$8 - 5 =$ ☐

$7 \times 4 =$ ☐

$14 - 8 =$ ☐

$2 \times 5 =$ ☐

$9 + 3 =$ ☐

$5 - 2 =$ ☐

$1 + 8 =$ ☐

$7 + 5 =$ ☐

$12 - 8 =$ ☐

$9 \times 8 =$ ☐

End Time ☐ : ☐

Date ☐ M ☐ D

Start Time ☐ : ☐

$4 + 9 =$ ☐

$4 - 3 =$ ☐

$13 - 5 =$ ☐

$9 + 0 =$ ☐

$2 \times 6 =$ ☐

$7 + 3 =$ ☐

$8 - 1 =$ ☐

$7 \times 7 =$ ☐

$11 - 5 =$ ☐

$8 \times 6 =$ ☐

$5 + 8 =$ ☐

$1 \times 6 =$ ☐

$3 + 4 =$ ☐

$12 - 8 =$ ☐

$6 + 6 =$ ☐

$7 \times 4 =$ ☐

$12 - 3 =$ ☐

$4 - 1 =$ ☐

$3 + 2 =$ ☐

$8 + 7 =$ ☐

$7 - 2 =$ ☐

$5 \times 3 =$ ☐

$14 - 9 =$ ☐

$7 + 5 =$ ☐

$6 \times 3 =$ ☐

$1 + 8 =$ ☐

$6 - 3 =$ ☐

$5 \times 9 =$ ☐

$11 - 6 =$ ☐

$8 \times 7 =$ ☐

$5 + 6 =$ ☐

$3 \times 2 =$ ☐

$15 - 9 =$ ☐

$4 \times 5 =$ ☐

$11 - 7 =$ ☐

$2 + 2 =$ ☐

$6 \times 6 =$ ☐

$4 - 4 =$ ☐

$3 + 6 =$ ☐

$10 - 7 =$ ☐

$7 \times 8 =$ ☐

$9 \times 5 =$ ☐

$2 + 4 =$ ☐

$9 + 8 =$ ☐

$0 \times 4 =$ ☐

$16 - 8 =$ ☐

$6 + 9 =$ ☐

$8 - 5 =$ ☐

$2 \times 7 =$ ☐

$3 + 9 =$ ☐

$6 \times 5 =$ [   ] $13 - 6 =$ [   ] $9 - 8 =$ [   ]

$9 + 4 =$ [   ] $8 \times 4 =$ [   ] $3 + 0 =$ [   ]

$14 - 6 =$ [   ] $7 + 7 =$ [   ] $8 \times 5 =$ [   ]

$3 \times 3 =$ [   ] $6 + 3 =$ [   ] $11 - 9 =$ [   ]

$11 - 2 =$ [   ] $9 \times 6 =$ [   ] $7 \times 6 =$ [   ]

$4 + 8 =$ [   ] $7 - 4 =$ [   ] $6 - 5 =$ [   ]

$3 + 5 =$ [   ] $1 + 7 =$ [   ] $9 \times 7 =$ [   ]

$5 - 4 =$ [   ] $5 - 3 =$ [   ] $6 + 8 =$ [   ]

$3 \times 6 =$ [   ] $7 \times 2 =$ [   ] $16 - 9 =$ [   ]

$7 + 9 =$ [   ] $10 - 9 =$ [   ] $3 \times 8 =$ [   ]

$9 - 9 =$ [   ] $5 + 8 =$ [   ] $5 + 2 =$ [   ]

$4 \times 7 =$ [   ] $6 \times 7 =$ [   ] $8 + 5 =$ [   ]

$2 + 6 =$ [   ] $9 + 2 =$ [   ] $14 - 7 =$ [   ]

$6 \times 4 =$ [   ] $5 \times 3 =$ [   ] $9 \times 4 =$ [   ]

$9 + 7 =$ [   ] $10 - 4 =$ [   ] $10 - 4 =$ [   ]

$15 - 8 =$ [   ] $8 + 3 =$ [   ] $7 \times 5 =$ [   ]

$9 \times 2 =$ [   ] $2 + 8 =$ [   ]

End Time [   ] : [   ]

I. Counting Test

Measure the time required for you to count from 1 to 120 aloud as fast as you can.

☐ sec.

II. Word Memorization Test

Memorize as many words as you can **within two minutes**.

fence	horse	baby	school	culture	mile
elastic	deal	world	rabbit	sign	land
act	page	group	flower	ocean	building
wing	dessert	chord	sun	interest	town
dollar	root	window	phrase	note	story

Write out as many words as you can remember **in two minutes** on the back of this page. How many words can you remember?

Number of words memorized ☐ words

Word Memorization Test Answers

III. Stroop Test

Please take the **Stroop Test** for Week 8, located on page **xi** of the Appendix.

Date ☐ M ☐ D

Start Time ☐ : ☐

$5 + 3 =$ ☐

$5 \times 7 =$ ☐

$4 \times 1 =$ ☐

$2 - 0 =$ ☐

$3 + 4 =$ ☐

$9 + 2 =$ ☐

$10 - 1 =$ ☐

$4 \times 5 =$ ☐

$15 - 8 =$ ☐

$7 - 5 =$ ☐

$3 \times 6 =$ ☐

$4 + 5 =$ ☐

$14 - 6 =$ ☐

$8 + 6 =$ ☐

$12 - 4 =$ ☐

$3 \times 9 =$ ☐

$5 \times 4 =$ ☐

$3 + 3 =$ ☐

$9 \times 9 =$ ☐

$5 - 4 =$ ☐

$2 \times 7 =$ ☐

$6 + 5 =$ ☐

$18 - 9 =$ ☐

$2 + 6 =$ ☐

$5 \times 6 =$ ☐

$9 \times 3 =$ ☐

$3 - 2 =$ ☐

$7 + 6 =$ ☐

$9 - 5 =$ ☐

$5 + 7 =$ ☐

$11 - 9 =$ ☐

$2 + 8 =$ ☐

$4 \times 6 =$ ☐

$12 - 5 =$ ☐

$8 \times 6 =$ ☐

$16 - 7 =$ ☐

$7 + 9 =$ ☐

$4 + 7 =$ ☐

$5 \times 5 =$ ☐

$3 + 5 =$ ☐

$3 \times 3 =$ ☐

$7 - 1 =$ ☐

$9 + 7 =$ ☐

$12 - 9 =$ ☐

$6 + 9 =$ ☐

$4 - 2 =$ ☐

$3 \times 5 =$ ☐

$3 + 1 =$ ☐

$2 \times 8 =$ ☐

$11 - 8 =$ ☐

$13 - 7 =$ [　]　　$4 + 2 =$ [　]　　$3 \times 8 =$ [　]

$3 + 2 =$ [　]　　$5 + 6 =$ [　]　　$9 \times 7 =$ [　]

$3 - 3 =$ [　]　　$9 - 9 =$ [　]　　$9 + 6 =$ [　]

$7 \times 2 =$ [　]　　$4 \times 8 =$ [　]　　$11 - 7 =$ [　]

$9 - 6 =$ [　]　　$9 + 8 =$ [　]　　$1 \times 9 =$ [　]

$10 - 5 =$ [　]　　$3 \times 7 =$ [　]　　$1 + 2 =$ [　]

$8 + 3 =$ [　]　　$11 - 2 =$ [　]　　$7 + 8 =$ [　]

$9 \times 4 =$ [　]　　$9 - 7 =$ [　]　　$13 - 9 =$ [　]

$2 + 4 =$ [　]　　$3 + 7 =$ [　]　　$8 \times 5 =$ [　]

$7 + 3 =$ [　]　　$9 \times 2 =$ [　]　　$9 \times 8 =$ [　]

$6 \times 2 =$ [　]　　$6 \times 9 =$ [　]　　$4 + 3 =$ [　]

$11 - 3 =$ [　]　　$0 + 7 =$ [　]　　$6 + 8 =$ [　]

$5 \times 9 =$ [　]　　$4 - 1 =$ [　]　　$5 - 2 =$ [　]

$12 - 7 =$ [　]　　$11 - 5 =$ [　]　　$7 \times 5 =$ [　]

$2 + 9 =$ [　]　　$3 + 9 =$ [　]　　$4 \times 4 =$ [　]

$7 \times 7 =$ [　]　　$5 \times 0 =$ [　]　　$14 - 5 =$ [　]

$15 - 6 =$ [　]　　$8 + 5 =$ [　]

End Time [　] : [　]

Start Time ☐ : ☐

7 + 2 = ☐

3 × 8 = ☐

9 + 9 = ☐

8 − 4 = ☐

2 × 2 = ☐

9 − 8 = ☐

8 + 0 = ☐

10 − 3 = ☐

6 × 3 = ☐

4 + 9 = ☐

6 + 7 = ☐

13 − 5 = ☐

4 × 8 = ☐

9 + 2 = ☐

18 − 9 = ☐

5 + 7 = ☐

14 − 9 = ☐

4 − 3 = ☐

1 + 8 = ☐

5 × 9 = ☐

8 + 6 = ☐

7 × 2 = ☐

9 − 5 = ☐

7 + 3 = ☐

13 − 6 = ☐

4 + 3 = ☐

7 × 9 = ☐

10 − 6 = ☐

3 + 9 = ☐

6 × 6 = ☐

5 − 3 = ☐

11 − 3 = ☐

2 × 9 = ☐

4 + 5 = ☐

16 − 8 = ☐

7 + 8 = ☐

3 × 6 = ☐

9 − 4 = ☐

1 × 5 = ☐

7 + 1 = ☐

2 × 6 = ☐

3 × 9 = ☐

5 − 5 = ☐

6 + 8 = ☐

4 × 7 = ☐

15 − 6 = ☐

5 × 2 = ☐

10 − 9 = ☐

9 × 3 = ☐

9 + 8 = ☐

$2 \times 5 =$ ☐

$6 - 4 =$ ☐

$14 - 7 =$ ☐

$3 + 5 =$ ☐

$8 + 3 =$ ☐

$5 \times 6 =$ ☐

$2 - 1 =$ ☐

$5 + 1 =$ ☐

$9 \times 7 =$ ☐

$7 + 6 =$ ☐

$10 - 8 =$ ☐

$6 + 5 =$ ☐

$14 - 5 =$ ☐

$9 \times 1 =$ ☐

$4 + 6 =$ ☐

$16 - 7 =$ ☐

$7 \times 3 =$ ☐

$5 \times 7 =$ ☐

$8 - 8 =$ ☐

$2 + 4 =$ ☐

$13 - 8 =$ ☐

$5 + 9 =$ ☐

$7 \times 5 =$ ☐

$6 \times 2 =$ ☐

$3 + 3 =$ ☐

$8 \times 7 =$ ☐

$6 - 3 =$ ☐

$5 \times 4 =$ ☐

$8 + 2 =$ ☐

$11 - 6 =$ ☐

$4 \times 4 =$ ☐

$12 - 8 =$ ☐

$7 + 5 =$ ☐

$15 - 9 =$ ☐

$2 + 5 =$ ☐

$3 \times 4 =$ ☐

$5 - 1 =$ ☐

$8 + 9 =$ ☐

$4 \times 9 =$ ☐

$3 + 4 =$ ☐

$11 - 8 =$ ☐

$4 \times 5 =$ ☐

$7 + 8 =$ ☐

$8 - 3 =$ ☐

$9 \times 9 =$ ☐

$12 - 6 =$ ☐

$1 + 9 =$ ☐

$8 \times 5 =$ ☐

$11 - 5 =$ ☐

$8 + 4 =$ ☐

End Time ☐ : ☐

Start Time ☐ : ☐

$2 \times 4 =$ ☐

$3 - 2 =$ ☐

$3 + 8 =$ ☐

$8 \times 6 =$ ☐

$7 + 0 =$ ☐

$3 \times 4 =$ ☐

$5 + 3 =$ ☐

$12 - 4 =$ ☐

$9 - 1 =$ ☐

$4 + 6 =$ ☐

$7 \times 3 =$ ☐

$13 - 4 =$ ☐

$10 - 3 =$ ☐

$9 \times 5 =$ ☐

$15 - 7 =$ ☐

$5 + 9 =$ ☐

$2 \times 3 =$ ☐

$1 + 5 =$ ☐

$7 - 2 =$ ☐

$6 \times 3 =$ ☐

$10 - 7 =$ ☐

$4 + 5 =$ ☐

$1 \times 9 =$ ☐

$6 - 4 =$ ☐

$8 \times 4 =$ ☐

$11 - 3 =$ ☐

$6 \times 4 =$ ☐

$3 + 9 =$ ☐

$8 \times 8 =$ ☐

$6 \times 7 =$ ☐

$6 + 4 =$ ☐

$13 - 6 =$ ☐

$9 + 3 =$ ☐

$3 + 4 =$ ☐

$13 - 8 =$ ☐

$2 + 2 =$ ☐

$2 \times 9 =$ ☐

$10 - 1 =$ ☐

$5 \times 5 =$ ☐

$9 + 2 =$ ☐

$6 - 5 =$ ☐

$6 + 2 =$ ☐

$9 - 7 =$ ☐

$7 \times 6 =$ ☐

$5 + 8 =$ ☐

$8 - 2 =$ ☐

$7 + 5 =$ ☐

$9 \times 2 =$ ☐

$6 + 8 =$ ☐

$17 - 9 =$ ☐

$6 \times 9 =$ ☐

$7 - 1 =$ ☐

$4 + 1 =$ ☐

$11 - 9 =$ ☐

$5 \times 0 =$ ☐

$8 + 5 =$ ☐

$9 \times 4 =$ ☐

$1 + 9 =$ ☐

$8 \times 5 =$ ☐

$9 + 4 =$ ☐

$5 - 1 =$ ☐

$11 - 7 =$ ☐

$2 + 8 =$ ☐

$3 \times 2 =$ ☐

$5 + 5 =$ ☐

$10 - 5 =$ ☐

$4 + 8 =$ ☐

$8 - 4 =$ ☐

$10 - 4 =$ ☐

$0 + 5 =$ ☐

$9 \times 8 =$ ☐

$12 - 3 =$ ☐

$7 \times 5 =$ ☐

$3 + 5 =$ ☐

$14 - 8 =$ ☐

$8 - 5 =$ ☐

$9 \times 3 =$ ☐

$15 - 6 =$ ☐

$9 + 7 =$ ☐

$3 \times 3 =$ ☐

$8 + 8 =$ ☐

$12 - 6 =$ ☐

$4 + 7 =$ ☐

$7 \times 9 =$ ☐

$1 + 0 =$ ☐

$7 - 4 =$ ☐

$3 \times 5 =$ ☐

$4 \times 9 =$ ☐

$7 + 6 =$ ☐

$9 \times 7 =$ ☐

$11 - 6 =$ ☐

$6 + 1 =$ ☐

$6 \times 5 =$ ☐

$8 + 9 =$ ☐

$8 - 7 =$ ☐

$4 \times 5 =$ ☐

$14 - 6 =$ ☐

$2 + 4 =$ ☐

$10 - 2 =$ ☐

$6 \times 2 =$ ☐

End Time ☐ : ☐

Date ☐ M ☐ D

Start Time ☐ : ☐

5 + 2 = ☐

3 × 5 = ☐

11 − 2 = ☐

9 + 2 = ☐

4 × 3 = ☐

9 − 9 = ☐

8 × 6 = ☐

1 + 7 = ☐

14 − 9 = ☐

5 + 8 = ☐

9 × 9 = ☐

3 + 6 = ☐

13 − 6 = ☐

9 × 6 = ☐

8 + 4 = ☐

15 − 6 = ☐

7 − 3 = ☐

8 − 2 = ☐

7 × 0 = ☐

2 + 6 = ☐

6 × 8 = ☐

7 + 4 = ☐

5 − 3 = ☐

12 − 7 = ☐

9 × 2 = ☐

5 × 1 = ☐

7 + 9 = ☐

6 + 8 = ☐

4 × 9 = ☐

3 + 0 = ☐

2 × 5 = ☐

3 × 8 = ☐

8 + 7 = ☐

9 × 7 = ☐

4 − 2 = ☐

4 + 5 = ☐

6 − 2 = ☐

3 × 3 = ☐

14 − 8 = ☐

3 + 5 = ☐

9 + 4 = ☐

9 − 3 = ☐

4 × 6 = ☐

12 − 9 = ☐

8 × 2 = ☐

8 + 6 = ☐

11 − 4 = ☐

3 + 9 = ☐

17 − 9 = ☐

9 × 3 = ☐

$3 - 2 =$ ☐ $5 \times 4 =$ ☐ $3 + 2 =$ ☐

$4 \times 5 =$ ☐ $8 - 3 =$ ☐ $7 + 8 =$ ☐

$3 + 7 =$ ☐ $6 + 7 =$ ☐ $3 \times 2 =$ ☐

$4 + 3 =$ ☐ $7 \times 2 =$ ☐ $9 - 6 =$ ☐

$6 \times 9 =$ ☐ $9 \times 4 =$ ☐ $5 + 7 =$ ☐

$6 + 5 =$ ☐ $3 + 1 =$ ☐ $3 \times 9 =$ ☐

$12 - 6 =$ ☐ $9 - 1 =$ ☐ $8 + 5 =$ ☐

$8 - 7 =$ ☐ $17 - 8 =$ ☐ $12 - 5 =$ ☐

$1 + 2 =$ ☐ $7 \times 7 =$ ☐ $2 + 5 =$ ☐

$8 \times 3 =$ ☐ $11 - 6 =$ ☐ $15 - 8 =$ ☐

$10 - 6 =$ ☐ $3 + 8 =$ ☐ $2 \times 9 =$ ☐

$3 \times 7 =$ ☐ $3 - 2 =$ ☐ $13 - 5 =$ ☐

$7 + 7 =$ ☐ $2 + 1 =$ ☐ $5 \times 3 =$ ☐

$5 \times 6 =$ ☐ $5 + 6 =$ ☐ $9 + 8 =$ ☐

$15 - 9 =$ ☐ $13 - 7 =$ ☐ $7 + 5 =$ ☐

$6 \times 2 =$ ☐ $6 \times 0 =$ ☐ $12 - 4 =$ ☐

$7 \times 9 =$ ☐ $12 - 3 =$ ☐

End Time ☐ : ☐

Date ☐ M ☐ D

Start Time ☐ : ☐

$7 - 3 =$ ☐

$3 + 6 =$ ☐

$8 + 4 =$ ☐

$9 - 8 =$ ☐

$1 \times 5 =$ ☐

$14 - 6 =$ ☐

$2 + 9 =$ ☐

$8 \times 7 =$ ☐

$4 + 2 =$ ☐

$7 - 4 =$ ☐

$3 \times 4 =$ ☐

$10 - 2 =$ ☐

$2 \times 9 =$ ☐

$5 + 7 =$ ☐

$4 \times 3 =$ ☐

$15 - 8 =$ ☐

$6 \times 8 =$ ☐

$14 - 5 =$ ☐

$1 + 3 =$ ☐

$2 \times 5 =$ ☐

$9 - 4 =$ ☐

$7 + 0 =$ ☐

$10 - 6 =$ ☐

$7 \times 3 =$ ☐

$2 \times 2 =$ ☐

$6 + 3 =$ ☐

$3 + 8 =$ ☐

$7 \times 8 =$ ☐

$12 - 9 =$ ☐

$4 + 7 =$ ☐

$8 - 2 =$ ☐

$6 \times 3 =$ ☐

$6 + 7 =$ ☐

$13 - 5 =$ ☐

$4 + 9 =$ ☐

$8 - 3 =$ ☐

$13 - 7 =$ ☐

$1 + 8 =$ ☐

$3 \times 3 =$ ☐

$7 + 4 =$ ☐

$4 - 3 =$ ☐

$6 \times 9 =$ ☐

$17 - 8 =$ ☐

$2 \times 4 =$ ☐

$7 + 6 =$ ☐

$8 \times 4 =$ ☐

$2 + 3 =$ ☐

$14 - 7 =$ ☐

$8 + 6 =$ ☐

$5 \times 3 =$ ☐

$10 - 8 =$ ☐ $6 - 2 =$ ☐ $4 \times 4 =$ ☐

$3 \times 9 =$ ☐ $5 + 0 =$ ☐ $8 + 9 =$ ☐

$8 + 8 =$ ☐ $9 \times 6 =$ ☐ $10 - 7 =$ ☐

$4 + 3 =$ ☐ $12 - 7 =$ ☐ $6 \times 6 =$ ☐

$5 \times 9 =$ ☐ $4 \times 7 =$ ☐ $3 \times 5 =$ ☐

$8 - 8 =$ ☐ $6 - 4 =$ ☐ $9 + 7 =$ ☐

$6 + 1 =$ ☐ $8 \times 3 =$ ☐ $3 + 4 =$ ☐

$5 - 3 =$ ☐ $8 + 5 =$ ☐ $7 - 0 =$ ☐

$8 \times 9 =$ ☐ $10 - 3 =$ ☐ $4 \times 9 =$ ☐

$11 - 5 =$ ☐ $9 \times 3 =$ ☐ $5 + 8 =$ ☐

$6 + 8 =$ ☐ $3 + 5 =$ ☐ $4 - 1 =$ ☐

$2 \times 3 =$ ☐ $9 + 4 =$ ☐ $9 \times 5 =$ ☐

$9 + 5 =$ ☐ $11 - 4 =$ ☐ $9 + 0 =$ ☐

$8 \times 2 =$ ☐ $5 \times 8 =$ ☐ $10 - 4 =$ ☐

$13 - 9 =$ ☐ $17 - 9 =$ ☐ $9 + 2 =$ ☐

$4 + 9 =$ ☐ $7 \times 1 =$ ☐ $14 - 7 =$ ☐

$6 \times 2 =$ ☐ $1 + 9 =$ ☐

End Time ☐ : ☐

I. Counting Test

Measure the time required for you to count from 1 to 120 aloud as fast as you can.

☐ sec.

II. Word Memorization Test

Memorize as many words as you can **within two minutes**.

peanut	amount	family	card	hour	ball
melon	sentence	rain	snake	team	parade
light	column	energy	spoon	ground	name
force	wave	body	object	money	river
door	travel	people	stop	cotton	melody

Write out as many words as you can remember **in two minutes** on the back of this page. How many words can you remember?

Number of words memorized ☐ words

Week 9

Word Memorization Test Answers

III. Stroop Test

Please take the **Stroop Test** for Week 9, located on page **xii** of the Appendix.

Start Time ☐ : ☐

$4 + 2 =$ ☐

$6 \times 4 =$ ☐

$5 - 3 =$ ☐

$2 + 9 =$ ☐

$13 - 9 =$ ☐

$1 \times 5 =$ ☐

$3 + 6 =$ ☐

$5 \times 7 =$ ☐

$7 - 4 =$ ☐

$4 \times 9 =$ ☐

$9 + 7 =$ ☐

$8 - 2 =$ ☐

$8 + 6 =$ ☐

$9 \times 9 =$ ☐

$16 - 8 =$ ☐

$0 \times 3 =$ ☐

$8 + 8 =$ ☐

$7 \times 3 =$ ☐

$12 - 9 =$ ☐

$8 + 3 =$ ☐

$4 - 4 =$ ☐

$7 + 6 =$ ☐

$3 + 2 =$ ☐

$8 \times 3 =$ ☐

$7 - 2 =$ ☐

$2 \times 8 =$ ☐

$14 - 9 =$ ☐

$6 + 7 =$ ☐

$2 \times 9 =$ ☐

$12 - 5 =$ ☐

$4 + 4 =$ ☐

$3 \times 5 =$ ☐

$9 + 8 =$ ☐

$4 \times 7 =$ ☐

$8 - 3 =$ ☐

$6 + 5 =$ ☐

$2 + 7 =$ ☐

$7 \times 1 =$ ☐

$9 + 5 =$ ☐

$16 - 7 =$ ☐

$1 + 1 =$ ☐

$8 \times 9 =$ ☐

$11 - 3 =$ ☐

$5 \times 6 =$ ☐

$2 - 1 =$ ☐

$5 + 4 =$ ☐

$11 - 4 =$ ☐

$5 \times 5 =$ ☐

$1 + 9 =$ ☐

$10 - 7 =$ ☐

$8 - 7 =$ ☐ $5 \times 2 =$ ☐ $3 + 4 =$ ☐

$8 + 4 =$ ☐ $10 - 6 =$ ☐ $9 - 1 =$ ☐

$3 + 3 =$ ☐ $8 + 2 =$ ☐ $2 \times 6 =$ ☐

$9 \times 3 =$ ☐ $13 - 7 =$ ☐ $11 - 5 =$ ☐

$6 + 8 =$ ☐ $6 - 5 =$ ☐ $3 + 9 =$ ☐

$3 \times 4 =$ ☐ $2 + 0 =$ ☐ $4 \times 5 =$ ☐

$10 - 2 =$ ☐ $8 \times 2 =$ ☐ $9 - 8 =$ ☐

$7 - 6 =$ ☐ $12 - 3 =$ ☐ $2 \times 4 =$ ☐

$6 + 9 =$ ☐ $4 + 6 =$ ☐ $1 + 7 =$ ☐

$2 \times 7 =$ ☐ $9 \times 0 =$ ☐ $8 + 5 =$ ☐

$5 - 1 =$ ☐ $2 + 3 =$ ☐ $3 \times 9 =$ ☐

$3 + 5 =$ ☐ $5 + 6 =$ ☐ $12 - 4 =$ ☐

$8 \times 8 =$ ☐ $6 - 3 =$ ☐ $7 \times 8 =$ ☐

$15 - 7 =$ ☐ $3 \times 8 =$ ☐ $10 - 9 =$ ☐

$9 + 6 =$ ☐ $16 - 9 =$ ☐ $9 + 1 =$ ☐

$3 \times 2 =$ ☐ $15 - 8 =$ ☐ $6 \times 8 =$ ☐

$11 - 6 =$ ☐ $6 \times 7 =$ ☐

End Time ☐ : ☐

Date ☐ M ☐ D

Start Time ☐ : ☐

$7 \times 7 =$ ☐

$6 - 3 =$ ☐

$2 + 5 =$ ☐

$7 + 4 =$ ☐

$5 \times 6 =$ ☐

$7 - 1 =$ ☐

$6 \times 4 =$ ☐

$10 - 8 =$ ☐

$6 + 3 =$ ☐

$9 \times 9 =$ ☐

$13 - 7 =$ ☐

$9 + 9 =$ ☐

$4 \times 2 =$ ☐

$8 - 4 =$ ☐

$15 - 9 =$ ☐

$8 + 8 =$ ☐

$10 - 6 =$ ☐

$5 + 2 =$ ☐

$6 \times 7 =$ ☐

$6 + 4 =$ ☐

$8 - 7 =$ ☐

$2 \times 8 =$ ☐

$7 + 2 =$ ☐

$11 - 9 =$ ☐

$8 \times 5 =$ ☐

$6 - 4 =$ ☐

$4 + 4 =$ ☐

$2 \times 1 =$ ☐

$8 + 4 =$ ☐

$3 \times 8 =$ ☐

$15 - 7 =$ ☐

$2 + 9 =$ ☐

$5 \times 5 =$ ☐

$8 \times 7 =$ ☐

$1 + 6 =$ ☐

$4 \times 3 =$ ☐

$14 - 9 =$ ☐

$9 + 7 =$ ☐

$9 \times 2 =$ ☐

$2 - 1 =$ ☐

$2 + 4 =$ ☐

$8 + 3 =$ ☐

$7 \times 2 =$ ☐

$3 + 5 =$ ☐

$11 - 4 =$ ☐

$12 - 7 =$ ☐

$7 + 6 =$ ☐

$5 \times 7 =$ ☐

$11 - 2 =$ ☐

$3 + 8 =$ ☐

$6 \times 5 =$ [ ] $2 + 3 =$ [ ] $1 - 1 =$ [ ]

$8 - 2 =$ [ ] $4 \times 5 =$ [ ] $14 - 7 =$ [ ]

$1 + 3 =$ [ ] $9 - 3 =$ [ ] $8 \times 8 =$ [ ]

$12 - 9 =$ [ ] $7 + 8 =$ [ ] $7 + 1 =$ [ ]

$5 + 8 =$ [ ] $2 \times 5 =$ [ ] $6 \times 5 =$ [ ]

$9 \times 5 =$ [ ] $0 + 4 =$ [ ] $3 \times 3 =$ [ ]

$2 + 8 =$ [ ] $11 - 3 =$ [ ] $7 - 4 =$ [ ]

$3 + 2 =$ [ ] $5 \times 8 =$ [ ] $5 + 1 =$ [ ]

$5 \times 4 =$ [ ] $4 + 8 =$ [ ] $9 + 8 =$ [ ]

$9 - 0 =$ [ ] $5 - 1 =$ [ ] $8 \times 1 =$ [ ]

$2 \times 3 =$ [ ] $10 - 3 =$ [ ] $16 - 9 =$ [ ]

$3 + 9 =$ [ ] $5 \times 1 =$ [ ] $7 + 9 =$ [ ]

$9 + 5 =$ [ ] $5 + 6 =$ [ ] $4 \times 7 =$ [ ]

$3 \times 7 =$ [ ] $8 \times 4 =$ [ ] $9 \times 8 =$ [ ]

$10 - 2 =$ [ ] $7 \times 8 =$ [ ] $8 + 5 =$ [ ]

$14 - 8 =$ [ ] $9 + 2 =$ [ ] $14 - 6 =$ [ ]

$11 - 6 =$ [ ] $11 - 5 =$ [ ]

End Time [ ] : [ ]

Date ☐ M ☐ D

Start Time ☐ : ☐

3 + 5 = ☐

9 + 6 = ☐

2 × 7 = ☐

6 × 2 = ☐

8 − 5 = ☐

3 + 2 = ☐

7 − 4 = ☐

15 − 8 = ☐

1 + 9 = ☐

4 × 6 = ☐

15 − 9 = ☐

3 × 4 = ☐

6 × 9 = ☐

7 + 6 = ☐

17 − 9 = ☐

9 × 4 = ☐

8 × 8 = ☐

11 − 3 = ☐

2 + 6 = ☐

7 − 1 = ☐

14 − 8 = ☐

3 × 3 = ☐

8 + 3 = ☐

0 × 8 = ☐

4 + 0 = ☐

2 × 2 = ☐

4 + 7 = ☐

2 × 5 = ☐

8 − 7 = ☐

3 + 9 = ☐

5 + 6 = ☐

4 × 5 = ☐

11 − 9 = ☐

5 + 4 = ☐

7 − 3 = ☐

8 × 2 = ☐

6 + 8 = ☐

3 × 7 = ☐

8 + 1 = ☐

6 × 6 = ☐

7 + 1 = ☐

17 − 8 = ☐

7 − 5 = ☐

6 + 9 = ☐

11 − 5 = ☐

5 × 4 = ☐

10 − 3 = ☐

7 × 5 = ☐

13 − 6 = ☐

8 + 8 = ☐

$4 - 0 =$ [ ]

$10 - 1 =$ [ ]

$6 + 3 =$ [ ]

$5 \times 5 =$ [ ]

$13 - 9 =$ [ ]

$7 \times 3 =$ [ ]

$2 + 1 =$ [ ]

$15 - 7 =$ [ ]

$5 - 3 =$ [ ]

$9 \times 3 =$ [ ]

$12 - 6 =$ [ ]

$3 + 7 =$ [ ]

$8 \times 3 =$ [ ]

$7 \times 6 =$ [ ]

$16 - 8 =$ [ ]

$9 + 7 =$ [ ]

$3 \times 9 =$ [ ]

$3 + 4 =$ [ ]

$6 - 4 =$ [ ]

$7 + 8 =$ [ ]

$6 \times 3 =$ [ ]

$8 + 6 =$ [ ]

$3 \times 2 =$ [ ]

$10 - 8 =$ [ ]

$0 + 3 =$ [ ]

$6 \times 7 =$ [ ]

$1 + 9 =$ [ ]

$5 - 2 =$ [ ]

$8 \times 9 =$ [ ]

$16 - 7 =$ [ ]

$8 + 0 =$ [ ]

$12 - 8 =$ [ ]

$3 \times 5 =$ [ ]

$7 + 9 =$ [ ]

$4 \times 2 =$ [ ]

$2 + 5 =$ [ ]

$7 - 6 =$ [ ]

$11 - 4 =$ [ ]

$5 \times 9 =$ [ ]

$15 - 6 =$ [ ]

$7 + 3 =$ [ ]

$5 + 5 =$ [ ]

$4 \times 3 =$ [ ]

$6 + 7 =$ [ ]

$9 - 5 =$ [ ]

$6 \times 8 =$ [ ]

$7 + 7 =$ [ ]

$9 \times 9 =$ [ ]

$4 + 8 =$ [ ]

$16 - 9 =$ [ ]

End Time [ ] : [ ]

Start Time ☐ : ☐

$5 \times 3 =$ ☐

$8 - 1 =$ ☐

$3 + 6 =$ ☐

$8 \times 4 =$ ☐

$7 + 5 =$ ☐

$9 - 8 =$ ☐

$5 + 4 =$ ☐

$3 \times 4 =$ ☐

$1 \times 7 =$ ☐

$8 + 7 =$ ☐

$6 + 6 =$ ☐

$14 - 5 =$ ☐

$2 \times 9 =$ ☐

$17 - 9 =$ ☐

$4 \times 5 =$ ☐

$7 + 4 =$ ☐

$2 + 5 =$ ☐

$7 - 2 =$ ☐

$9 \times 8 =$ ☐

$4 - 3 =$ ☐

$9 + 8 =$ ☐

$15 - 6 =$ ☐

$8 + 1 =$ ☐

$6 \times 8 =$ ☐

$9 - 5 =$ ☐

$2 \times 3 =$ ☐

$18 - 9 =$ ☐

$2 \times 5 =$ ☐

$7 + 6 =$ ☐

$13 - 4 =$ ☐

$8 + 2 =$ ☐

$10 - 7 =$ ☐

$5 \times 2 =$ ☐

$8 - 3 =$ ☐

$9 \times 7 =$ ☐

$3 + 5 =$ ☐

$13 - 5 =$ ☐

$8 + 6 =$ ☐

$6 \times 7 =$ ☐

$9 - 4 =$ ☐

$5 \times 6 =$ ☐

$3 + 1 =$ ☐

$10 - 9 =$ ☐

$6 + 9 =$ ☐

$4 + 5 =$ ☐

$8 \times 9 =$ ☐

$16 - 7 =$ ☐

$4 \times 7 =$ ☐

$9 + 5 =$ ☐

$12 - 8 =$ ☐

$6 \times 3 =$ [ ] $4 + 4 =$ [ ] $8 - 2 =$ [ ]

$5 + 8 =$ [ ] $3 + 9 =$ [ ] $4 + 1 =$ [ ]

$12 - 9 =$ [ ] $2 \times 4 =$ [ ] $6 + 8 =$ [ ]

$8 - 6 =$ [ ] $7 - 4 =$ [ ] $2 + 7 =$ [ ]

$4 \times 3 =$ [ ] $8 + 4 =$ [ ] $7 \times 9 =$ [ ]

$9 - 3 =$ [ ] $3 + 0 =$ [ ] $10 - 1 =$ [ ]

$1 + 3 =$ [ ] $9 \times 9 =$ [ ] $8 + 7 =$ [ ]

$7 \times 6 =$ [ ] $11 - 5 =$ [ ] $6 - 6 =$ [ ]

$17 - 8 =$ [ ] $7 + 7 =$ [ ] $1 + 6 =$ [ ]

$8 \times 5 =$ [ ] $13 - 9 =$ [ ] $5 \times 9 =$ [ ]

$7 + 9 =$ [ ] $5 \times 7 =$ [ ] $10 - 4 =$ [ ]

$6 - 3 =$ [ ] $5 + 9 =$ [ ] $2 \times 8 =$ [ ]

$2 \times 7 =$ [ ] $9 \times 2 =$ [ ] $6 + 4 =$ [ ]

$9 + 3 =$ [ ] $16 - 8 =$ [ ] $3 \times 8 =$ [ ]

$16 - 9 =$ [ ] $4 + 9 =$ [ ] $11 - 4 =$ [ ]

$5 \times 8 =$ [ ] $15 - 6 =$ [ ] $3 \times 9 =$ [ ]

$14 - 7 =$ [ ] $4 \times 8 =$ [ ]

End Time [ ] : [ ]

Date ☐ M ☐ D

Start Time ☐ : ☐

2 + 1 =

6 + 9 =

7 × 6 =

8 − 2 =

13 − 4 =

6 + 2 =

7 − 2 =

0 × 7 =

2 + 4 =

6 × 5 =

5 + 7 =

12 − 8 =

9 × 9 =

11 − 7 =

3 × 1 =

2 + 9 =

6 × 6 =

7 + 3 =

5 − 1 =

8 + 7 =

10 − 5 =

8 × 7 =

6 + 8 =

4 × 5 =

7 − 7 =

11 − 8 =

2 × 9 =

9 + 1 =

2 × 4 =

3 + 6 =

9 × 4 =

7 + 4 =

11 − 4 =

12 − 3 =

6 − 2 =

4 + 2 =

9 + 2 =

8 − 6 =

7 × 3 =

17 − 9 =

9 − 1 =

4 × 7 =

2 + 6 =

4 + 9 =

2 × 6 =

12 − 9 =

4 × 3 =

5 + 5 =

18 − 9 =

9 × 7 =

6 − 1 = ☐   4 + 6 = ☐   12 − 6 = ☐

3 + 5 = ☐   9 × 0 = ☐   3 + 9 = ☐

4 × 9 = ☐   15 − 9 = ☐   8 × 2 = ☐

7 × 2 = ☐   3 × 5 = ☐   9 + 0 = ☐

8 − 7 = ☐   9 + 9 = ☐   8 × 8 = ☐

10 − 9 = ☐   16 − 7 = ☐   2 − 1 = ☐

2 × 3 = ☐   3 + 0 = ☐   4 + 5 = ☐

9 + 5 = ☐   6 − 4 = ☐   7 − 6 = ☐

15 − 7 = ☐   9 × 2 = ☐   12 − 5 = ☐

4 × 8 = ☐   8 + 3 = ☐   4 × 6 = ☐

1 + 4 = ☐   8 − 5 = ☐   7 + 5 = ☐

7 + 9 = ☐   7 × 7 = ☐   8 × 6 = ☐

11 − 3 = ☐   7 + 2 = ☐   5 + 6 = ☐

6 × 4 = ☐   3 × 8 = ☐   14 − 8 = ☐

10 − 2 = ☐   7 × 9 = ☐   6 + 7 = ☐

8 × 3 = ☐   4 + 8 = ☐   6 × 3 = ☐

5 + 9 = ☐   10 − 6 = ☐

End Time ☐ : ☐

I. Counting Test

Measure the time required for you to count from 1 to 120 aloud as fast as you can.

☐ sec.

II. Word Memorization Test

Memorize as many words as you can **within two minutes**.

sea	back	art	hill	pound	verb
catch	sense	father	wood	afternoon	tone
guest	design	storage	coat	web	fish
record	plant	neighbor	star	linen	method
test	meal	doctor	product	speed	craft

Write out as many words as you can remember **in two minutes** on the back of this page. How many words can you remember?

Number of words memorized ☐ words

Word Memorization Test Answers

III. Stroop Test

Please take the **Stroop Test** for Week 10, located on page **xiii** of the Appendix.

Date ☐ M ☐ D

Start Time ☐ : ☐

$6 \times 5 =$ ☐

$9 - 9 =$ ☐

$7 + 3 =$ ☐

$6 - 2 =$ ☐

$8 + 6 =$ ☐

$2 + 2 =$ ☐

$9 \times 9 =$ ☐

$8 - 6 =$ ☐

$1 \times 7 =$ ☐

$10 - 3 =$ ☐

$4 + 6 =$ ☐

$6 \times 9 =$ ☐

$12 - 6 =$ ☐

$3 + 5 =$ ☐

$2 \times 6 =$ ☐

$8 + 8 =$ ☐

$4 \times 3 =$ ☐

$9 - 8 =$ ☐

$6 + 4 =$ ☐

$5 + 3 =$ ☐

$7 + 4 =$ ☐

$8 + 9 =$ ☐

$13 - 4 =$ ☐

$2 + 6 =$ ☐

$7 \times 2 =$ ☐

$11 - 5 =$ ☐

$5 \times 7 =$ ☐

$3 - 2 =$ ☐

$4 + 5 =$ ☐

$10 - 9 =$ ☐

$8 \times 4 =$ ☐

$9 + 5 =$ ☐

$13 - 7 =$ ☐

$9 \times 5 =$ ☐

$6 + 1 =$ ☐

$5 \times 5 =$ ☐

$9 - 5 =$ ☐

$6 + 6 =$ ☐

$10 - 8 =$ ☐

$6 \times 7 =$ ☐

$2 + 5 =$ ☐

$4 \times 8 =$ ☐

$4 - 1 =$ ☐

$5 \times 2 =$ ☐

$3 + 8 =$ ☐

$7 - 4 =$ ☐

$8 \times 9 =$ ☐

$8 + 5 =$ ☐

$15 - 6 =$ ☐

$9 \times 3 =$ ☐

$3 \times 5 =$ [   ]　　$3 + 6 =$ [   ]　　$7 - 1 =$ [   ]

$16 - 9 =$ [   ]　　$7 - 5 =$ [   ]　　$9 + 8 =$ [   ]

$6 + 7 =$ [   ]　　$5 \times 9 =$ [   ]　　$5 + 0 =$ [   ]

$9 \times 1 =$ [   ]　　$13 - 5 =$ [   ]　　$7 \times 9 =$ [   ]

$8 - 5 =$ [   ]　　$6 + 8 =$ [   ]　　$5 + 8 =$ [   ]

$4 + 4 =$ [   ]　　$8 \times 3 =$ [   ]　　$3 \times 7 =$ [   ]

$3 \times 6 =$ [   ]　　$9 - 3 =$ [   ]　　$13 - 8 =$ [   ]

$10 - 4 =$ [   ]　　$7 \times 4 =$ [   ]　　$9 - 6 =$ [   ]

$5 + 6 =$ [   ]　　$1 + 7 =$ [   ]　　$2 \times 7 =$ [   ]

$3 \times 4 =$ [   ]　　$9 + 2 =$ [   ]　　$2 + 8 =$ [   ]

$1 + 5 =$ [   ]　　$1 \times 1 =$ [   ]　　$1 - 1 =$ [   ]

$9 + 4 =$ [   ]　　$11 - 3 =$ [   ]　　$2 + 4 =$ [   ]

$4 - 2 =$ [   ]　　$9 \times 7 =$ [   ]　　$11 - 4 =$ [   ]

$7 \times 8 =$ [   ]　　$17 - 9 =$ [   ]　　$13 - 6 =$ [   ]

$11 - 9 =$ [   ]　　$7 + 5 =$ [   ]　　$9 + 1 =$ [   ]

$17 - 8 =$ [   ]　　$9 \times 4 =$ [   ]　　$6 \times 8 =$ [   ]

$14 - 9 =$ [   ]　　$2 \times 2 =$ [   ]

End Time [   ] : [   ]

Start Time ☐ : ☐

$3 + 5 =$ ☐

$8 \times 7 =$ ☐

$9 + 1 =$ ☐

$4 - 4 =$ ☐

$1 \times 8 =$ ☐

$2 + 6 =$ ☐

$14 - 9 =$ ☐

$3 \times 4 =$ ☐

$6 - 3 =$ ☐

$4 + 5 =$ ☐

$6 \times 6 =$ ☐

$8 + 4 =$ ☐

$2 \times 6 =$ ☐

$10 - 7 =$ ☐

$3 + 9 =$ ☐

$5 \times 8 =$ ☐

$5 \times 5 =$ ☐

$2 + 6 =$ ☐

$2 \times 3 =$ ☐

$14 - 5 =$ ☐

$6 + 5 =$ ☐

$4 \times 1 =$ ☐

$9 - 3 =$ ☐

$8 + 1 =$ ☐

$14 - 8 =$ ☐

$6 \times 5 =$ ☐

$4 + 3 =$ ☐

$17 - 8 =$ ☐

$16 - 9 =$ ☐

$2 + 8 =$ ☐

$7 \times 8 =$ ☐

$13 - 6 =$ ☐

$8 + 7 =$ ☐

$6 \times 3 =$ ☐

$1 \times 6 =$ ☐

$8 - 5 =$ ☐

$5 + 2 =$ ☐

$7 + 4 =$ ☐

$4 \times 8 =$ ☐

$9 - 6 =$ ☐

$9 \times 5 =$ ☐

$13 - 4 =$ ☐

$3 + 6 =$ ☐

$2 \times 7 =$ ☐

$11 - 5 =$ ☐

$9 + 5 =$ ☐

$7 \times 5 =$ ☐

$9 - 2 =$ ☐

$15 - 7 =$ ☐

$1 + 9 =$ ☐

$5 + 1 =$ [　]　　$4 - 2 =$ [　]　　$9 \times 6 =$ [　]

$7 \times 3 =$ [　]　　$16 - 8 =$ [　]　　$7 - 6 =$ [　]

$3 - 3 =$ [　]　　$3 \times 2 =$ [　]　　$6 + 3 =$ [　]

$9 + 2 =$ [　]　　$1 + 6 =$ [　]　　$15 - 9 =$ [　]

$8 \times 6 =$ [　]　　$2 \times 4 =$ [　]　　$9 + 3 =$ [　]

$2 + 3 =$ [　]　　$9 \times 1 =$ [　]　　$7 \times 4 =$ [　]

$13 - 7 =$ [　]　　$8 - 3 =$ [　]　　$8 + 5 =$ [　]

$7 \times 9 =$ [　]　　$4 + 4 =$ [　]　　$3 + 4 =$ [　]

$6 + 9 =$ [　]　　$9 + 7 =$ [　]　　$9 \times 9 =$ [　]

$5 - 1 =$ [　]　　$5 \times 6 =$ [　]　　$9 - 5 =$ [　]

$11 - 4 =$ [　]　　$13 - 9 =$ [　]　　$8 \times 3 =$ [　]

$2 \times 9 =$ [　]　　$8 + 8 =$ [　]　　$8 + 6 =$ [　]

$3 + 7 =$ [　]　　$3 \times 6 =$ [　]　　$8 + 3 =$ [　]

$4 \times 4 =$ [　]　　$6 \times 7 =$ [　]　　$3 \times 9 =$ [　]

$12 - 7 =$ [　]　　$7 + 7 =$ [　]　　$10 - 9 =$ [　]

$9 + 2 =$ [　]　　$11 - 8 =$ [　]　　$16 - 7 =$ [　]

$14 - 7 =$ [　]　　$12 - 5 =$ [　]

End Time [ ] : [ ]

Date [ ] M [ ] D

Start Time [ ] : [ ]

$12 - 6 =$ [ ]

$6 + 2 =$ [ ]

$3 - 2 =$ [ ]

$13 - 8 =$ [ ]

$4 \times 3 =$ [ ]

$9 + 6 =$ [ ]

$3 \times 3 =$ [ ]

$8 + 1 =$ [ ]

$4 - 3 =$ [ ]

$4 + 8 =$ [ ]

$5 \times 1 =$ [ ]

$9 - 3 =$ [ ]

$7 + 8 =$ [ ]

$6 + 5 =$ [ ]

$7 \times 3 =$ [ ]

$17 - 9 =$ [ ]

$2 + 7 =$ [ ]

$4 - 0 =$ [ ]

$6 \times 7 =$ [ ]

$9 + 7 =$ [ ]

$8 \times 0 =$ [ ]

$1 + 3 =$ [ ]

$7 \times 9 =$ [ ]

$3 + 5 =$ [ ]

$5 + 8 =$ [ ]

$9 - 4 =$ [ ]

$3 + 7 =$ [ ]

$12 - 3 =$ [ ]

$3 \times 2 =$ [ ]

$10 - 6 =$ [ ]

$8 \times 7 =$ [ ]

$12 - 4 =$ [ ]

$2 + 8 =$ [ ]

$9 \times 8 =$ [ ]

$1 + 6 =$ [ ]

$6 + 7 =$ [ ]

$3 \times 8 =$ [ ]

$9 \times 7 =$ [ ]

$9 - 1 =$ [ ]

$6 + 3 =$ [ ]

$6 - 2 =$ [ ]

$10 - 1 =$ [ ]

$8 + 3 =$ [ ]

$3 \times 7 =$ [ ]

$11 - 9 =$ [ ]

$9 \times 6 =$ [ ]

$2 \times 6 =$ [ ]

$7 + 3 =$ [ ]

$18 - 9 =$ [ ]

$4 \times 7 =$ [ ]

5 + 1 = [ ]   2 × 7 = [ ]   2 − 1 = [ ]

7 − 7 = [ ]   7 + 2 = [ ]   10 − 9 = [ ]

9 + 1 = [ ]   6 − 1 = [ ]   5 + 4 = [ ]

6 × 5 = [ ]   17 − 8 = [ ]   3 × 6 = [ ]

8 + 7 = [ ]   8 × 1 = [ ]   11 − 3 = [ ]

9 × 3 = [ ]   11 − 4 = [ ]   6 × 8 = [ ]

10 − 5 = [ ]   1 + 9 = [ ]   3 + 3 = [ ]

0 + 6 = [ ]   3 + 8 = [ ]   15 − 6 = [ ]

5 × 7 = [ ]   9 × 5 = [ ]   7 − 5 = [ ]

4 + 6 = [ ]   7 + 4 = [ ]   2 × 8 = [ ]

7 − 4 = [ ]   9 − 8 = [ ]   9 + 9 = [ ]

2 × 2 = [ ]   2 × 4 = [ ]   13 − 9 = [ ]

15 − 8 = [ ]   7 + 9 = [ ]   4 × 6 = [ ]

4 + 3 = [ ]   4 × 6 = [ ]   8 × 6 = [ ]

11 − 7 = [ ]   9 + 2 = [ ]   10 − 7 = [ ]

5 × 5 = [ ]   14 − 9 = [ ]   6 + 9 = [ ]

8 + 4 = [ ]   7 × 4 = [ ]

End Time [ ] : [ ]

Day 54

Start Time ☐ : ☐

8 − 3 = ☐

9 × 4 = ☐

3 − 2 = ☐

6 + 9 = ☐

12 − 4 = ☐

2 + 1 = ☐

3 × 2 = ☐

6 − 4 = ☐

5 × 2 = ☐

13 − 9 = ☐

8 × 5 = ☐

7 + 2 = ☐

14 − 7 = ☐

8 + 7 = ☐

13 − 5 = ☐

6 × 5 = ☐

4 − 3 = ☐

4 × 8 = ☐

2 + 7 = ☐

17 − 9 = ☐

3 + 7 = ☐

1 × 9 = ☐

8 − 7 = ☐

2 × 4 = ☐

3 + 6 = ☐

10 − 3 = ☐

8 + 4 = ☐

4 + 3 = ☐

9 × 5 = ☐

14 − 9 = ☐

4 × 4 = ☐

2 + 9 = ☐

11 − 7 = ☐

3 + 3 = ☐

9 × 2 = ☐

4 − 4 = ☐

7 × 5 = ☐

4 + 2 = ☐

1 + 9 = ☐

5 − 1 = ☐

6 + 2 = ☐

8 × 4 = ☐

5 × 6 = ☐

7 + 9 = ☐

4 + 8 = ☐

10 − 5 = ☐

9 × 7 = ☐

11 − 8 = ☐

3 × 5 = ☐

8 + 6 = ☐

$2 + 2 =$ ☐

$6 + 8 =$ ☐

$7 \times 2 =$ ☐

$9 - 4 =$ ☐

$1 + 7 =$ ☐

$8 + 1 =$ ☐

$6 \times 3 =$ ☐

$11 - 8 =$ ☐

$4 + 6 =$ ☐

$16 - 9 =$ ☐

$3 \times 7 =$ ☐

$9 + 4 =$ ☐

$8 \times 2 =$ ☐

$15 - 6 =$ ☐

$7 + 4 =$ ☐

$12 - 8 =$ ☐

$2 \times 9 =$ ☐

$6 - 1 =$ ☐

$5 + 4 =$ ☐

$9 + 3 =$ ☐

$2 + 5 =$ ☐

$9 \times 6 =$ ☐

$10 - 8 =$ ☐

$6 + 4 =$ ☐

$9 - 5 =$ ☐

$3 + 4 =$ ☐

$2 \times 2 =$ ☐

$13 - 6 =$ ☐

$2 \times 5 =$ ☐

$8 + 5 =$ ☐

$7 \times 6 =$ ☐

$14 - 5 =$ ☐

$5 \times 8 =$ ☐

$17 - 8 =$ ☐

$5 \times 9 =$ ☐

$4 + 8 =$ ☐

$15 - 7 =$ ☐

$5 - 3 =$ ☐

$4 \times 6 =$ ☐

$7 - 2 =$ ☐

$5 + 3 =$ ☐

$6 \times 8 =$ ☐

$13 - 8 =$ ☐

$9 \times 3 =$ ☐

$9 + 5 =$ ☐

$8 - 6 =$ ☐

$5 \times 3 =$ ☐

$6 + 6 =$ ☐

$10 - 4 =$ ☐

$4 \times 5 =$ ☐

End Time ☐ : ☐

Date [ ] M [ ] D

Start Time [ ] : [ ]

$1 + 3 =$

$6 - 5 =$

$5 + 7 =$

$11 - 8 =$

$3 \times 7 =$

$9 + 8 =$

$6 \times 9 =$

$9 - 5 =$

$15 - 7 =$

$3 \times 3 =$

$3 + 9 =$

$8 \times 6 =$

$5 + 3 =$

$7 \times 8 =$

$9 + 4 =$

$10 - 6 =$

$16 - 8 =$

$4 - 1 =$

$7 + 2 =$

$5 + 6 =$

$8 - 7 =$

$4 \times 9 =$

$6 \times 2 =$

$7 - 2 =$

$3 \times 6 =$

$6 + 0 =$

$9 + 9 =$

$6 \times 5 =$

$16 - 7 =$

$7 \times 3 =$

$2 + 8 =$

$11 - 5 =$

$2 \times 3 =$

$3 \times 9 =$

$4 + 2 =$

$7 + 9 =$

$8 \times 5 =$

$9 - 1 =$

$12 - 8 =$

$4 + 5 =$

$8 - 3 =$

$9 \times 8 =$

$1 + 2 =$

$0 \times 7 =$

$9 + 3 =$

$11 - 2 =$

$8 \times 3 =$

$14 - 6 =$

$9 \times 7 =$

$5 + 8 =$

$9 + 6 =$ [ ]

$4 \times 5 =$ [ ]

$11 - 9 =$ [ ]

$5 \times 8 =$ [ ]

$5 + 5 =$ [ ]

$12 - 3 =$ [ ]

$6 + 2 =$ [ ]

$7 - 1 =$ [ ]

$8 \times 8 =$ [ ]

$4 + 7 =$ [ ]

$4 - 2 =$ [ ]

$2 \times 5 =$ [ ]

$5 + 1 =$ [ ]

$4 \times 3 =$ [ ]

$5 \times 6 =$ [ ]

$2 + 9 =$ [ ]

$12 - 5 =$ [ ]

$10 - 1 =$ [ ]

$3 + 7 =$ [ ]

$9 \times 2 =$ [ ]

$5 + 4 =$ [ ]

$3 \times 8 =$ [ ]

$7 - 3 =$ [ ]

$1 + 6 =$ [ ]

$14 - 7 =$ [ ]

$6 - 4 =$ [ ]

$7 \times 7 =$ [ ]

$9 + 1 =$ [ ]

$3 \times 4 =$ [ ]

$8 + 9 =$ [ ]

$12 - 7 =$ [ ]

$4 + 6 =$ [ ]

$5 \times 3 =$ [ ]

$6 + 6 =$ [ ]

$8 - 0 =$ [ ]

$3 + 6 =$ [ ]

$4 \times 2 =$ [ ]

$9 \times 4 =$ [ ]

$6 - 2 =$ [ ]

$14 - 8 =$ [ ]

$7 \times 4 =$ [ ]

$5 + 8 =$ [ ]

$11 - 4 =$ [ ]

$4 \times 6 =$ [ ]

$3 + 1 =$ [ ]

$8 + 7 =$ [ ]

$13 - 5 =$ [ ]

$6 \times 6 =$ [ ]

$11 - 9 =$ [ ]

$9 \times 3 =$ [ ]

End Time [ ] : [ ]

I. Counting Test

Measure the time required for you to count from 1 to 120 aloud as fast as you can.

☐ sec.

II. Word Memorization Test

Memorize as many words as you can **within two minutes**.

shape	past	article	milk	shell	feet
relish	play	bird	car	raisin	dirt
result	south	love	brick	grass	theme
fine	house	sound	power	cook	moment
arm	vote	diary	state	cat	pumpkin

Write out as many words as you can remember **in two minutes** on the back of this page. How many words can you remember?

Number of words memorized ☐ words

143

Word Memorization Test Answers

III. Stroop Test

Please take the **Stroop Test** for Week 11, located on page **xiv** of the Appendix.

Start Time ☐ : ☐

$8 - 7 =$ ☐

$7 + 9 =$ ☐

$3 + 3 =$ ☐

$3 \times 7 =$ ☐

$5 + 5 =$ ☐

$10 - 6 =$ ☐

$1 + 8 =$ ☐

$7 \times 6 =$ ☐

$11 - 5 =$ ☐

$5 \times 2 =$ ☐

$3 - 1 =$ ☐

$0 + 2 =$ ☐

$12 - 8 =$ ☐

$6 \times 3 =$ ☐

$2 + 9 =$ ☐

$4 \times 4 =$ ☐

$7 \times 2 =$ ☐

$3 + 5 =$ ☐

$14 - 7 =$ ☐

$7 - 1 =$ ☐

$4 + 6 =$ ☐

$10 - 8 =$ ☐

$5 \times 6 =$ ☐

$6 + 1 =$ ☐

$5 \times 8 =$ ☐

$8 - 2 =$ ☐

$7 \times 1 =$ ☐

$9 + 2 =$ ☐

$7 - 4 =$ ☐

$5 + 7 =$ ☐

$3 \times 4 =$ ☐

$13 - 5 =$ ☐

$6 \times 9 =$ ☐

$11 - 9 =$ ☐

$3 \times 6 =$ ☐

$15 - 8 =$ ☐

$2 + 8 =$ ☐

$9 - 2 =$ ☐

$8 + 5 =$ ☐

$3 + 4 =$ ☐

$2 \times 7 =$ ☐

$5 - 4 =$ ☐

$9 \times 8 =$ ☐

$10 - 3 =$ ☐

$8 + 2 =$ ☐

$6 \times 5 =$ ☐

$14 - 6 =$ ☐

$3 + 1 =$ ☐

$5 \times 4 =$ ☐

$6 + 6 =$ ☐

$6 + 2 =$ ☐ $5 - 1 =$ ☐ $8 \times 5 =$ ☐

$8 - 4 =$ ☐ $7 + 8 =$ ☐ $11 - 2 =$ ☐

$3 \times 5 =$ ☐ $3 + 0 =$ ☐ $5 + 9 =$ ☐

$10 - 4 =$ ☐ $4 \times 7 =$ ☐ $14 - 8 =$ ☐

$9 + 6 =$ ☐ $5 + 6 =$ ☐ $6 - 2 =$ ☐

$8 \times 8 =$ ☐ $9 \times 6 =$ ☐ $3 + 3 =$ ☐

$1 - 1 =$ ☐ $12 - 7 =$ ☐ $6 \times 2 =$ ☐

$2 \times 2 =$ ☐ $8 - 3 =$ ☐ $16 - 7 =$ ☐

$4 + 2 =$ ☐ $7 + 6 =$ ☐ $3 + 7 =$ ☐

$8 + 6 =$ ☐ $4 \times 5 =$ ☐ $9 \times 5 =$ ☐

$7 \times 3 =$ ☐ $6 - 4 =$ ☐ $1 + 5 =$ ☐

$13 - 8 =$ ☐ $2 + 7 =$ ☐ $9 + 4 =$ ☐

$8 \times 7 =$ ☐ $5 \times 9 =$ ☐ $9 - 3 =$ ☐

$11 - 3 =$ ☐ $11 - 6 =$ ☐ $12 - 4 =$ ☐

$4 + 7 =$ ☐ $8 + 8 =$ ☐ $13 - 6 =$ ☐

$8 \times 2 =$ ☐ $7 \times 5 =$ ☐ $18 - 9 =$ ☐

$3 \times 9 =$ ☐ $16 - 9 =$ ☐

End Time [ ] : [ ]

Date ☐ M ☐ D

Start Time ☐ : ☐

1 + 6 = ☐

4 × 8 = ☐

16 − 9 = ☐

3 + 8 = ☐

9 × 3 = ☐

6 − 5 = ☐

7 + 1 = ☐

5 + 5 = ☐

1 × 6 = ☐

4 + 4 = ☐

13 − 9 = ☐

17 − 8 = ☐

9 + 3 = ☐

6 × 3 = ☐

12 − 4 = ☐

6 + 8 = ☐

9 × 7 = ☐

6 × 9 = ☐

8 − 3 = ☐

2 + 0 = ☐

9 + 5 = ☐

3 × 3 = ☐

9 − 3 = ☐

5 × 7 = ☐

17 − 9 = ☐

3 + 6 = ☐

9 × 0 = ☐

10 − 8 = ☐

8 + 4 = ☐

9 × 6 = ☐

5 − 3 = ☐

9 + 6 = ☐

15 − 8 = ☐

11 − 3 = ☐

3 + 4 = ☐

6 × 7 = ☐

8 + 5 = ☐

7 − 5 = ☐

9 × 8 = ☐

5 + 4 = ☐

11 − 7 = ☐

8 × 5 = ☐

7 − 4 = ☐

0 + 9 = ☐

2 × 4 = ☐

7 + 7 = ☐

2 × 6 = ☐

10 − 5 = ☐

3 + 9 = ☐

7 × 7 = ☐

6 − 1 = [ ]   6 × 8 = [ ]   7 + 2 = [ ]

11 − 8 = [ ]   8 − 4 = [ ]   5 × 8 = [ ]

4 × 9 = [ ]   0 + 3 = [ ]   9 − 6 = [ ]

4 + 5 = [ ]   9 × 4 = [ ]   2 + 8 = [ ]

7 × 4 = [ ]   8 + 7 = [ ]   3 × 9 = [ ]

8 × 6 = [ ]   6 × 5 = [ ]   3 + 2 = [ ]

9 − 7 = [ ]   2 + 1 = [ ]   15 − 9 = [ ]

2 + 7 = [ ]   8 + 9 = [ ]   8 × 3 = [ ]

8 + 8 = [ ]   4 × 6 = [ ]   4 + 6 = [ ]

3 × 6 = [ ]   8 − 1 = [ ]   7 − 2 = [ ]

12 − 8 = [ ]   8 × 3 = [ ]   14 − 7 = [ ]

5 + 9 = [ ]   2 + 9 = [ ]   3 × 4 = [ ]

8 × 4 = [ ]   7 + 5 = [ ]   6 + 7 = [ ]

6 × 1 = [ ]   8 × 7 = [ ]   5 × 4 = [ ]

9 + 9 = [ ]   12 − 3 = [ ]   13 − 8 = [ ]

10 − 1 = [ ]   18 − 9 = [ ]   4 + 7 = [ ]

12 − 9 = [ ]   11 − 2 = [ ]

End Time [ ] : [ ]

Date ☐ M ☐ D

Start Time ☐ : ☐

$7 - 0 =$ ☐

$8 \times 5 =$ ☐

$6 + 6 =$ ☐

$9 \times 7 =$ ☐

$4 + 1 =$ ☐

$2 \times 6 =$ ☐

$5 + 3 =$ ☐

$10 - 1 =$ ☐

$8 - 2 =$ ☐

$5 + 9 =$ ☐

$13 - 5 =$ ☐

$7 \times 3 =$ ☐

$11 - 4 =$ ☐

$2 \times 3 =$ ☐

$15 - 9 =$ ☐

$8 + 5 =$ ☐

$1 + 7 =$ ☐

$3 + 6 =$ ☐

$9 + 8 =$ ☐

$2 \times 4 =$ ☐

$0 + 5 =$ ☐

$2 - 1 =$ ☐

$3 + 3 =$ ☐

$8 - 4 =$ ☐

$11 - 5 =$ ☐

$9 + 2 =$ ☐

$7 \times 4 =$ ☐

$10 - 5 =$ ☐

$1 \times 9 =$ ☐

$8 \times 6 =$ ☐

$8 + 4 =$ ☐

$11 - 7 =$ ☐

$9 \times 5 =$ ☐

$5 \times 7 =$ ☐

$11 - 8 =$ ☐

$6 + 2 =$ ☐

$4 - 1 =$ ☐

$16 - 7 =$ ☐

$8 \times 8 =$ ☐

$4 + 8 =$ ☐

$3 \times 7 =$ ☐

$2 + 5 =$ ☐

$7 - 7 =$ ☐

$8 + 9 =$ ☐

$5 \times 4 =$ ☐

$6 - 5 =$ ☐

$6 + 4 =$ ☐

$4 + 9 =$ ☐

$7 \times 6 =$ ☐

$16 - 9 =$ ☐

$6 \times 4 =$ [ ] $9 - 7 =$ [ ] $2 + 2 =$ [ ]

$1 + 0 =$ [ ] $10 - 6 =$ [ ] $8 - 4 =$ [ ]

$7 - 3 =$ [ ] $2 + 4 =$ [ ] $2 + 9 =$ [ ]

$11 - 9 =$ [ ] $7 \times 7 =$ [ ] $5 \times 2 =$ [ ]

$7 \times 1 =$ [ ] $12 - 9 =$ [ ] $8 + 8 =$ [ ]

$14 - 6 =$ [ ] $9 \times 8 =$ [ ] $7 \times 2 =$ [ ]

$5 + 5 =$ [ ] $4 + 3 =$ [ ] $12 - 3 =$ [ ]

$9 + 7 =$ [ ] $12 - 6 =$ [ ] $5 + 2 =$ [ ]

$4 \times 8 =$ [ ] $7 - 1 =$ [ ] $2 \times 9 =$ [ ]

$7 + 3 =$ [ ] $4 \times 3 =$ [ ] $7 + 8 =$ [ ]

$8 - 1 =$ [ ] $16 - 8 =$ [ ] $5 - 1 =$ [ ]

$5 \times 6 =$ [ ] $9 + 4 =$ [ ] $4 \times 6 =$ [ ]

$6 + 8 =$ [ ] $6 \times 6 =$ [ ] $10 - 2 =$ [ ]

$8 \times 7 =$ [ ] $3 \times 5 =$ [ ] $5 + 4 =$ [ ]

$7 + 4 =$ [ ] $13 - 9 =$ [ ] $17 - 8 =$ [ ]

$18 - 9 =$ [ ] $3 + 8 =$ [ ] $3 \times 2 =$ [ ]

$5 + 6 =$ [ ] $9 \times 4 =$ [ ]

End Time [ ] : [ ]

Day 59

Start Time ☐ : ☐

8 × 2 = ☐

4 + 5 = ☐

10 − 5 = ☐

9 + 4 = ☐

2 × 7 = ☐

7 − 7 = ☐

9 × 2 = ☐

2 + 3 = ☐

16 − 8 = ☐

7 + 4 = ☐

4 + 2 = ☐

9 × 8 = ☐

11 − 5 = ☐

7 × 1 = ☐

8 + 8 = ☐

14 − 7 = ☐

4 − 1 = ☐

2 × 3 = ☐

7 − 6 = ☐

2 + 1 = ☐

6 × 2 = ☐

6 + 7 = ☐

9 − 2 = ☐

3 + 4 = ☐

8 × 7 = ☐

3 × 3 = ☐

5 + 9 = ☐

9 + 3 = ☐

12 − 6 = ☐

9 × 7 = ☐

10 − 8 = ☐

5 × 4 = ☐

9 + 1 = ☐

3 + 3 = ☐

5 − 2 = ☐

8 × 8 = ☐

3 − 2 = ☐

7 + 9 = ☐

12 − 8 = ☐

1 + 5 = ☐

9 × 4 = ☐

8 − 2 = ☐

9 × 3 = ☐

13 − 5 = ☐

7 × 8 = ☐

6 + 4 = ☐

10 − 2 = ☐

7 + 3 = ☐

15 − 6 = ☐

5 × 9 = ☐

$6 - 3 =$ ☐

$3 + 2 =$ ☐

$5 + 7 =$ ☐

$1 + 8 =$ ☐

$4 \times 3 =$ ☐

$13 - 7 =$ ☐

$8 + 3 =$ ☐

$6 - 5 =$ ☐

$6 + 2 =$ ☐

$3 \times 6 =$ ☐

$13 - 4 =$ ☐

$7 \times 3 =$ ☐

$2 + 9 =$ ☐

$6 \times 5 =$ ☐

$10 - 7 =$ ☐

$2 \times 8 =$ ☐

$7 \times 7 =$ ☐

$2 \times 4 =$ ☐

$4 + 8 =$ ☐

$11 - 6 =$ ☐

$7 - 2 =$ ☐

$4 \times 5 =$ ☐

$5 - 4 =$ ☐

$2 + 7 =$ ☐

$8 \times 4 =$ ☐

$15 - 7 =$ ☐

$2 \times 8 =$ ☐

$8 + 5 =$ ☐

$4 - 2 =$ ☐

$5 \times 5 =$ ☐

$3 + 9 =$ ☐

$12 - 5 =$ ☐

$5 \times 7 =$ ☐

$16 - 9 =$ ☐

$5 + 0 =$ ☐

$9 + 5 =$ ☐

$4 \times 9 =$ ☐

$9 - 2 =$ ☐

$6 + 8 =$ ☐

$2 + 6 =$ ☐

$7 \times 9 =$ ☐

$11 - 3 =$ ☐

$4 + 7 =$ ☐

$14 - 8 =$ ☐

$5 \times 2 =$ ☐

$7 + 8 =$ ☐

$2 \times 9 =$ ☐

$12 - 7 =$ ☐

$6 + 5 =$ ☐

$17 - 8 =$ ☐

End Time ☐ : ☐

Date ☐ M ☐ D

Start Time ☐ : ☐

$8 - 5 =$ ☐

$1 + 6 =$ ☐

$3 + 7 =$ ☐

$9 - 1 =$ ☐

$3 \times 5 =$ ☐

$10 - 7 =$ ☐

$8 - 3 =$ ☐

$5 \times 7 =$ ☐

$3 + 4 =$ ☐

$8 + 2 =$ ☐

$5 + 6 =$ ☐

$11 - 6 =$ ☐

$6 \times 4 =$ ☐

$8 + 9 =$ ☐

$14 - 7 =$ ☐

$4 \times 5 =$ ☐

$5 \times 4 =$ ☐

$4 + 3 =$ ☐

$7 - 5 =$ ☐

$9 \times 6 =$ ☐

$8 - 6 =$ ☐

$12 - 3 =$ ☐

$4 + 4 =$ ☐

$8 - 2 =$ ☐

$2 \times 7 =$ ☐

$6 + 2 =$ ☐

$4 \times 9 =$ ☐

$3 + 8 =$ ☐

$10 - 9 =$ ☐

$2 \times 3 =$ ☐

$15 - 7 =$ ☐

$8 \times 9 =$ ☐

$9 + 1 =$ ☐

$3 \times 9 =$ ☐

$4 + 8 =$ ☐

$8 - 1 =$ ☐

$5 + 7 =$ ☐

$15 - 9 =$ ☐

$4 \times 4 =$ ☐

$9 + 3 =$ ☐

$8 \times 2 =$ ☐

$6 - 4 =$ ☐

$4 \times 8 =$ ☐

$13 - 5 =$ ☐

$8 + 4 =$ ☐

$6 \times 3 =$ ☐

$2 + 6 =$ ☐

$7 \times 7 =$ ☐

$6 + 4 =$ ☐

$11 - 2 =$ ☐

$13 - 7 =$ [ ] $4 - 2 =$ [ ] $6 + 6 =$ [ ]

$8 + 6 =$ [ ] $9 + 0 =$ [ ] $3 \times 4 =$ [ ]

$8 \times 3 =$ [ ] $13 - 7 =$ [ ] $12 - 8 =$ [ ]

$2 + 1 =$ [ ] $9 \times 2 =$ [ ] $5 \times 5 =$ [ ]

$4 \times 7 =$ [ ] $9 - 4 =$ [ ] $3 + 9 =$ [ ]

$3 - 3 =$ [ ] $11 - 9 =$ [ ] $10 - 6 =$ [ ]

$6 + 3 =$ [ ] $7 \times 3 =$ [ ] $5 + 1 =$ [ ]

$9 - 6 =$ [ ] $1 + 9 =$ [ ] $9 - 8 =$ [ ]

$11 - 5 =$ [ ] $12 - 7 =$ [ ] $2 \times 9 =$ [ ]

$2 \times 8 =$ [ ] $9 \times 3 =$ [ ] $9 + 5 =$ [ ]

$7 + 6 =$ [ ] $5 + 4 =$ [ ] $3 - 1 =$ [ ]

$5 \times 6 =$ [ ] $9 + 9 =$ [ ] $5 \times 2 =$ [ ]

$4 + 9 =$ [ ] $10 - 4 =$ [ ] $3 + 6 =$ [ ]

$10 - 1 =$ [ ] $8 \times 8 =$ [ ] $12 - 4 =$ [ ]

$8 + 8 =$ [ ] $14 - 9 =$ [ ] $7 + 5 =$ [ ]

$7 \times 1 =$ [ ] $3 \times 2 =$ [ ] $8 \times 7 =$ [ ]

$17 - 8 =$ [ ] $9 + 7 =$ [ ]

End Time [ ] : [ ]

I. Counting Test

Measure the time required for you to count from 1 to 120 aloud as fast as you can.

☐ sec.

II. Word Memorization Test

Memorize as many words as you can **within two minutes.**

rice	thing	cent	band	dime	eye
list	nation	field	stamp	example	air
board	poem	ink	garden	wind	right
value	swim	pole	mouth	dress	quart
work	finger	morning	side	dance	boat

Write out as many words as you can remember **in two minutes** on the back of this page. How many words can you remember?

Number of words memorized ☐ words

Word Memorization Test Answers

III. Stroop Test

Please take the **Stroop Test** for Week 12, located on page **xv** of the Appendix.

Answers

21

Day 5 — Date M D | Time | Start Time

7−2=5	13−6=7	4+7=11
1+3=4	5×7=35	3+5=8
6×9=54	3+9=12	4×8=32
3×1=3	7×6=42	12−6=6
5+9=14	8−2=6	2+8=10
2×6=12	4+0=4	7−3=4
16−8=8	7+9=16	5+4=9
9+6=15	3×6=18	0×0=0
5−5=0	15−8=7	13−8=5
7×9=63	3+3=6	5×3=15
14−5=9	7+6=13	3+6=9
7−1=6	12−5=7	10−4=6
2×4=8	8×7=56	9−9=0
3+8=11	9−0=9	8+9=17
9×3=27	3×8=24	15−6=9
9+1=10	4×4=16	2×8=16
	4+8=12	2+4=6

Day 5 — | | Time Required | End Time

4×6=24	2+5=7	11−9=2
2+9=11	17−9=8	7+7=14
11−3=8	7×4=28	3×2=6
9×8=72	8+2=10	14−6=8
2−2=0	2×8=16	7×8=56
6+7=13	13−7=6	6+9=15
13−5=8	8×1=8	7−5=2
3+9=12	4+4=8	4+3=7
4×3=12	9×6=54	10−8=2
5−4=1	8+3=11	9×5=45
8×9=72	5×2=10	2+6=8
8−5=3	10−5=5	16−9=7
7+8=15	2+7=9	5−4=1
1+6=7	4×7=28	6×7=42
13−9=4	12−4=8	9+4=13
3×6=18	6+8=14	18−9=9
5×5=25	8−3=5	

Day 6 — Date M D | | Start Time

8+2=10	7−2=5	4×8=32
11−4=7	3+3=6	1+5=6
2+5=7	4×3=12	5×3=15
6×4=24	9×3=27	5−0=5
18−9=9	8+4=12	6+8=14
7+5=12	16−7=9	12−7=5
7−7=0	3×2=6	4×1=4
5+8=13	7+1=8	8−3=5
9×7=63	9+9=18	3×7=21
6−4=2	6×6=36	6+1=7
7×2=14	14−6=8	10−9=1
10−5=5	7×8=56	6×2=12
6+5=11	9−5=4	5+7=12
2×9=18	4+5=9	5×5=45
8+0=8	6×7=42	7×7=49
5−3=2	11−2=9	12−9=3
	9+1=10	9+3=12

26

Day 6 — | | Time Required | End Time

2×7=14	9+8=17	6−5=1
5−1=4	4×2=8	5+5=10
1+4=5	5+7=12	3×8=24
9×9=81	9−3=6	14−9=5
2+8=10	14−5=9	8×2=16
3+4=7	7×6=42	13−4=9
11−8=3	12−3=9	3+6=9
2×1=2	1+9=10	10−1=9
5×4=20	6×3=18	8−6=2
7+6=13	4+8=12	6×5=30
6−6=0	7−0=7	3+9=12
17−8=9	4+2=6	14−7=7
3×9=27	7+7=14	6×8=48
2+2=4	4×6=24	5+4=9
15−8=7	2×5=10	4+9=13
4×4=16	11−9=2	13−6=7
8+6=14	5×5=25	

Day 7 — Date M D | | Start Time

14−9=5	5×2=10	5+7=12
5×8=40	6+1=7	9×8=72
9+3=12	11−6=5	17−9=8
11−2=9	1+9=10	5+2=7
6×2=12	9×3=27	8+2=10
0×7=0	8−7=1	5×5=25
2+6=8	6+5=11	2×8=16
12−4=8	9−4=5	8+5=13
7−2=5	2×9=18	9−8=1
4+8=12	5×7=35	13−7=6
2×1=2	12−7=5	6×5=30
10−2=8	2+4=6	1+5=6
4−1=3	7−4=3	3×2=6
3+2=5	3+9=12	6−4=2
8×3=24	7×6=42	9+8=17
7+3=10	15−8=7	4+5=9
	4×6=24	12−9=3

28

Day 7 — | | Time Required | End Time

3×5=15	6−3=3	9+7=16
11−7=4	9+2=11	3×0=0
4+6=10	13−5=8	5−5=0
4×3=12	6×4=24	7+0=7
13−5=8	9×1=9	16−7=9
2×4=8	6+5=11	5+8=13
6+9=15	8×6=48	9×5=45
1+7=8	13−9=4	6+2=8
10−9=1	8+1=9	9−5=4
7+4=11	9×2=18	10−8=2
6×2=12	7+6=13	8×7=56
8+7=15	6×2=12	8−4=4
7−2=5	8+7=15	7+2=9
2×5=10	7−3=...	9+1=10
3−2=1	18−9=9	10−8=2
4×9=36	4×8=32	7+9=16
14−6=8	4×7=28	

Day 8 — Date M D | | Start Time

2×5=10	7−4=3	8+9=17
15−6=9	3×5=15	12−3=9
6×4=24	12−8=4	7+5=12
4+9=13	7+2=9	4×8=32
8−2=6	4×3=12	8×6=48
4×9=36	1−1=0	13−4=9
6+4=10	9+4=13	1+8=9
11−7=4	3×2=6	8×9=72
6×3=18	14−6=8	6+6=12
3+5=8	3+3=6	9−7=2
8+7=15	2×4=8	8×5=40
1×6=6	2+6=8	9×2=18
10−2=8	2×7=14	11−6=5
4−3=1	14−8=6	3×7=21
7+4=11	9+1=10	5−3=2
6×6=36	10−7=3	2+8=10
8−6=2		

30

Day 8 — | | Time Required | End Time

9−5=4	13−9=3	7×2=14
3+7=10	2×0=0	15−8=7
1×6=6	6+5=11	1+6=7
4+2=6	3+6=9	6×2=12
5×9=45	14−5=9	5×8=40
8+4=12	4+7=11	7+9=16
9×7=63	7×5=35	7−6=1
14−6=8	3−3=0	4×2=8
1+9=10	5+5=10	6×8=48
8×7=56	3×3=9	15−9=6
2×3=6	10−3=7	2+5=7
10−7=3	3+1=4	6+9=15
3+9=12	3×9=27	9−3=6
3−2=1	5+7=12	7+8=15
6×5=30	12−6=6	16−7=9
12−9=3	5×6=30	7×8=56
2+1=3	8−7=1	

Day 9 (page 31) — M D Date / Start Time

5 × 3 = 15	8 + 7 = 15	10 − 2 = 8
2 + 8 = 10	5 + 0 = 5	9 + 6 = 15
11 − 3 = 8	9 × 4 = 36	4 − 1 = 3
4 × 2 = 8	12 − 9 = 3	5 × 6 = 30
1 + 9 = 10	4 + 7 = 11	12 − 3 = 9
9 × 3 = 27	9 − 0 = 9	1 + 8 = 9
5 − 4 = 1	4 × 7 = 28	7 − 2 = 5
5 + 2 = 7	15 − 9 = 6	6 + 9 = 15
8 × 2 = 16	6 + 3 = 9	8 × 3 = 24
10 − 8 = 2	12 − 5 = 7	11 − 4 = 7
8 + 5 = 13	1 × 8 = 8	4 × 5 = 20
4 × 6 = 24	1 + 2 = 3	6 − 1 = 1
5 × 9 = 45	9 − 5 = 4	6 + 6 = 12
1 + 5 = 6	15 − 7 = 8	4 × 8 = 32
8 − 3 = 5	7 × 4 = 28	13 − 8 = 5
9 + 8 = 17	4 × 0 = 0	7 + 2 = 9
3 × 7 = 21	9 + 7 = 16	

Day 9 (page 32) — Time Required / End Time

7 − 3 = 4	16 − 7 = 9	2 + 9 = 11
2 × 9 = 18	8 × 6 = 48	5 × 1 = 5
7 + 6 = 13	8 − 8 = 0	18 − 9 = 9
3 × 2 = 6	5 + 6 = 11	6 + 0 = 6
16 − 8 = 8	8 × 4 = 32	10 − 9 = 1
3 + 5 = 8	12 − 7 = 5	7 + 6 = 13
7 × 9 = 63	7 × 7 = 49	7 × 3 = 21
8 + 4 = 12	9 + 9 = 18	7 − 4 = 3
17 − 9 = 8	15 − 8 = 7	3 + 7 = 10
8 × 7 = 56	3 − 1 = 2	5 × 5 = 25
13 − 5 = 8	2 × 2 = 4	9 − 3 = 6
8 + 1 = 9	4 + 3 = 7	3 × 8 = 24
7 + 9 = 16	9 + 2 = 11	5 + 4 = 9
9 × 6 = 54	4 × 9 = 36	10 − 3 = 7
5 × 7 = 35	9 + 0 = 9	9 + 5 = 14
14 − 9 = 5	11 − 8 = 3	6 × 4 = 24
	7 + 7 = 14	3 − 3 = 0

Day 10 (page 33) — M D Date / Start Time

13 − 8 = 5	8 + 5 = 13	9 × 2 = 18
3 + 4 = 7	2 + 6 = 8	2 + 8 = 10
3 × 9 = 27	9 × 5 = 45	5 × 7 = 35
7 × 0 = 0	10 − 9 = 1	9 − 2 = 7
8 × 6 = 48	9 + 3 = 12	3 + 0 = 3
1 + 9 = 10	7 − 2 = 5	5 + 7 = 12
5 × 9 = 45	7 + 1 = 8	4 × 1 = 4
10 − 3 = 7	2 × 6 = 12	12 − 6 = 6
7 + 8 = 15	16 − 9 = 7	8 + 1 = 9
7 − 3 = 4	4 × 8 = 32	9 + 4 = 13
6 × 3 = 18	8 + 7 = 15	13 − 6 = 7
17 − 9 = 8	5 × 4 = 20	3 × 7 = 21
3 − 1 = 2	9 − 8 = 1	7 − 1 = 6
7 × 6 = 42	7 + 3 = 10	5 × 6 = 30
9 + 2 = 11	10 − 5 = 5	2 × 6 = 12
8 × 4 = 32	6 × 9 = 54	9 + 6 = 15
11 − 8 = 3	4 + 4 = 8	

Day 10 (page 34) — Time Required / End Time

3 × 5 = 15	11 − 2 = 9	8 + 1 = 9
7 + 5 = 12	3 + 8 = 11	13 − 7 = 6
10 − 2 = 8	6 × 9 = 54	5 × 2 = 10
9 × 8 = 72	12 − 5 = 7	2 + 9 = 11
8 − 8 = 0	2 × 4 = 8	8 × 5 = 40
3 + 9 = 12	8 + 9 = 17	12 − 7 = 5
13 − 4 = 9	9 − 1 = 8	4 × 6 = 24
5 + 5 = 10	2 + 4 = 6	1 + 2 = 3
4 × 2 = 8	14 − 8 = 6	8 × 0 = 0
9 − 6 = 3	1 × 9 = 9	6 + 7 = 13
7 × 8 = 56	6 + 3 = 9	7 × 2 = 14
7 − 7 = 0	7 + 9 = 16	16 − 8 = 8
6 + 6 = 12	6 − 2 = 4	3 + 2 = 5
4 + 3 = 7	9 × 4 = 36	6 × 7 = 42
11 − 5 = 6	5 + 8 = 13	18 − 9 = 9
9 × 3 = 27	11 − 4 = 7	9 + 2 = 11
	5 × 5 = 25	6 − 5 = 1

Day 11 (page 37) — M D Date / Start Time

3 × 1 = 3	8 − 8 = 0	3 + 2 = 5
4 + 7 = 11	5 + 2 = 7	4 × 9 = 36
18 − 9 = 9	9 × 0 = 0	3 × 6 = 18
3 + 4 = 7	6 − 3 = 3	7 + 3 = 10
6 × 6 = 36	7 + 4 = 11	10 − 2 = 8
15 − 7 = 8	11 − 9 = 2	2 × 9 = 18
5 + 7 = 12	5 × 2 = 10	5 + 3 = 8
8 − 7 = 1	4 − 2 = 2	2 + 8 = 10
2 × 3 = 6	3 × 2 = 6	13 − 8 = 5
9 × 5 = 45	6 + 3 = 9	12 − 9 = 3
9 − 4 = 5	14 − 7 = 7	6 × 9 = 54
3 × 9 = 27	5 × 6 = 30	7 − 2 = 5
15 − 8 = 7	8 + 5 = 13	4 + 1 = 5
6 + 6 = 12	4 × 9 = 36	4 × 4 = 16
7 × 9 = 63	8 × 9 = 72	11 − 6 = 5
7 + 0 = 7	14 − 5 = 9	8 + 7 = 15
6 − 1 = 5	9 + 7 = 16	

Day 11 (page 38) — Time Required / End Time

6 × 2 = 12	9 − 7 = 2	7 + 6 = 13
7 − 6 = 1	8 + 6 = 14	8 × 5 = 40
3 + 6 = 9	5 × 5 = 25	4 + 6 = 10
5 × 3 = 15	14 − 6 = 8	7 − 1 = 6
4 + 8 = 12	1 × 1 = 1	13 − 7 = 6
2 + 1 = 3	10 − 1 = 9	6 × 8 = 48
11 − 7 = 4	3 + 0 = 3	12 − 7 = 5
9 × 1 = 9	5 × 1 = 5	5 + 9 = 14
5 × 4 = 20	8 − 7 = 1	3 × 4 = 12
9 + 6 = 15	4 × 6 = 24	15 − 9 = 6
6 − 5 = 1	7 + 5 = 12	5 − 0 = 5
14 − 8 = 6	12 − 3 = 9	2 + 7 = 9
3 × 8 = 24	8 × 6 = 48	8 + 9 = 17
3 + 5 = 8	1 + 5 = 6	9 × 4 = 36
13 − 4 = 9	9 + 4 = 13	9 × 8 = 72
3 × 6 = 18	16 − 9 = 7	10 − 3 = 7
	7 × 2 = 14	9 + 2 = 11

Day 12 (page 39) — M D Date / Start Time

8 + 6 = 14	5 × 8 = 40	7 + 2 = 9
11 − 9 = 2	7 × 8 = 56	11 − 5 = 6
8 × 3 = 24	10 − 9 = 1	4 + 8 = 12
5 + 8 = 13	4 + 3 = 7	4 × 2 = 8
13 − 8 = 5	8 + 9 = 17	5 × 7 = 35
3 × 7 = 21	9 × 3 = 27	9 + 5 = 14
8 × 8 = 64	6 × 8 = 48	8 × 7 = 56
9 + 0 = 9	4 + 6 = 10	12 − 3 = 9
15 − 6 = 9	6 − 2 = 4	8 + 0 = 8
6 − 1 = 5	6 × 6 = 36	4 × 7 = 28
6 + 6 = 12	9 × 2 = 18	6 + 7 = 13
9 × 7 = 63	16 − 7 = 9	13 − 4 = 7
14 − 5 = 9	3 + 6 = 9	2 × 9 = 18
9 − 8 = 1	5 − 3 = 2	11 − 8 = 3
3 + 4 = 7	5 + 9 = 14	3 × 6 = 18
1 × 6 = 6	6 × 8 = 48	7 + 6 = 13
4 + 7 = 11	3 × 3 = 9	15 − 7 = 8

Day 12 (page 40) — Time Required / End Time

3 × 9 = 27	9 + 2 = 11	7 − 3 = 4
16 − 9 = 7	6 × 5 = 30	8 + 4 = 12
1 + 9 = 10	8 − 2 = 6	11 − 4 = 7
1 × 2 = 2	1 + 4 = 5	4 × 2 = 8
11 − 7 = 4	12 − 5 = 7	5 × 7 = 35
9 × 8 = 72	4 + 9 = 13	9 + 5 = 14
7 + 8 = 15	4 × 6 = 24	8 × 7 = 56
5 + 4 = 9	5 + 1 = 6	12 − 3 = 9
13 − 7 = 6	7 − 1 = 6	8 + 0 = 8
3 + 1 = 4	17 − 8 = 9	4 × 7 = 28
9 × 9 = 81	8 × 5 = 40	6 + 7 = 13
8 + 4 = 12	9 − 2 = 7	13 − 4 = 7
9 − 2 = 7	1 + 6 = 7	2 × 9 = 18
7 × 5 = 35	14 − 6 = 8	11 − 8 = 3
4 − 4 = 0	4 + 8 = 12	3 × 6 = 18
7 × 4 = 28	7 + 9 = 16	7 + 6 = 13
	0 × 7 = 0	15 − 7 = 8

Day 21 — Date M D — Start Time

13 − 9 = 4	4 + 0 = 4	9 × 9 = 81
1 + 2 = 3	7 × 4 = 28	5 + 2 = 7
8 + 8 = 16	9 − 5 = 4	8 − 3 = 5
12 − 8 = 4	4 × 5 = 20	6 × 4 = 24
9 × 4 = 36	8 + 7 = 15	15 − 7 = 8
7 + 8 = 15	4 + 4 = 8	3 × 5 = 15
5 − 3 = 2	8 × 5 = 40	7 + 6 = 13
4 + 6 = 10	14 − 6 = 8	6 − 5 = 1
6 − 2 = 4	9 + 7 = 16	5 × 4 = 20
7 × 3 = 21	2 × 9 = 18	8 × 4 = 32
8 + 4 = 12	5 − 5 = 0	10 − 1 = 9
17 − 9 = 8	4 × 2 = 8	1 × 9 = 9
9 × 6 = 54	13 − 9 = 4	5 + 7 = 12
6 × 5 = 30	3 + 6 = 9	7 × 7 = 49
2 + 7 = 9	7 × 9 = 63	2 + 5 = 7
8 − 5 = 3	12 − 5 = 7	11 − 3 = 8
	6 + 8 = 14	9 + 1 = 10

Day 21 — Time Required — End Time

2 × 4 = 8	3 + 0 = 3	8 − 7 = 1
7 − 2 = 5	7 × 8 = 56	5 × 6 = 30
1 + 4 = 5	8 + 6 = 14	4 + 6 = 10
9 × 1 = 9	9 − 6 = 3	13 − 5 = 8
7 + 9 = 16	12 − 4 = 8	9 × 5 = 45
4 × 8 = 32	9 + 5 = 14	13 − 7 = 6
13 − 4 = 9	8 × 2 = 16	4 + 5 = 9
2 + 2 = 4	6 + 8 = 14	2 × 7 = 14
4 × 9 = 36	3 × 9 = 27	8 − 8 = 0
5 + 9 = 14	6 + 4 = 10	9 × 2 = 18
12 − 6 = 6	9 − 1 = 8	8 + 2 = 10
5 × 7 = 35	12 − 9 = 3	10 − 8 = 2
3 − 2 = 1	9 + 3 = 12	6 × 8 = 48
3 + 5 = 8	6 × 7 = 42	6 + 2 = 8
10 − 4 = 6	5 × 3 = 15	12 − 7 = 5
2 × 3 = 6	14 − 7 = 7	9 + 6 = 15
7 + 3 = 10	6 × 3 = 18	

Day 22 — Date M D — Start Time

6 + 6 = 12	5 × 7 = 35	15 − 7 = 8
6 × 3 = 18	0 + 5 = 5	6 × 8 = 48
3 + 9 = 12	13 − 5 = 8	2 + 4 = 6
11 − 6 = 5	6 + 5 = 11	14 − 8 = 6
4 × 9 = 36	8 × 3 = 24	3 + 8 = 11
1 + 7 = 8	9 − 1 = 8	9 × 9 = 81
3 × 7 = 21	9 + 9 = 18	4 × 7 = 28
1 + 9 = 10	8 − 2 = 6	9 + 2 = 11
9 − 6 = 3	9 × 8 = 72	9 − 8 = 1
13 − 4 = 9	3 × 6 = 18	5 × 2 = 10
2 × 3 = 6	5 + 4 = 9	13 − 8 = 5
12 − 4 = 8	11 − 3 = 8	7 + 0 = 7
7 − 2 = 5	7 + 5 = 12	8 × 7 = 56
2 + 6 = 8	4 × 3 = 12	5 + 8 = 13
2 × 9 = 18	1 − 1 = 0	7 − 4 = 3
6 + 7 = 13	10 − 9 = 1	4 + 3 = 7
	8 × 5 = 40	12 − 6 = 6

Day 22 — Time Required — End Time

7 × 2 = 14	13 − 7 = 6	8 + 9 = 17
12 − 8 = 4	4 + 8 = 12	2 × 7 = 14
9 + 7 = 16	8 − 5 = 3	5 + 3 = 8
3 × 8 = 24	6 × 6 = 36	4 − 1 = 3
2 × 6 = 12	3 − 2 = 1	11 − 2 = 9
17 − 9 = 8	5 + 5 = 10	8 + 3 = 11
5 + 6 = 11	7 × 8 = 56	9 × 7 = 63
13 − 5 = 8	10 − 6 = 4	8 − 4 = 4
6 + 2 = 8	7 + 2 = 9	4 + 1 = 5
16 − 8 = 8	14 − 5 = 9	5 × 5 = 25
9 × 4 = 36	9 × 1 = 9	12 − 5 = 7
8 + 8 = 16	4 + 7 = 11	6 − 3 = 3
5 − 2 = 3	3 × 0 = 0	3 + 2 = 5
3 + 6 = 9	10 − 3 = 7	11 − 8 = 3
8 × 4 = 32	4 × 5 = 20	6 + 4 = 10
15 − 9 = 6	9 + 7 = 16	9 × 5 = 45
4 × 6 = 24	7 + 6 = 13	

Day 23 — Date M D — Start Time

8 + 6 = 14	14 − 8 = 6	3 × 7 = 21
3 − 2 = 1	8 − 6 = 2	15 − 8 = 7
12 − 6 = 6	3 × 3 = 9	6 + 4 = 10
3 + 5 = 8	2 + 9 = 11	5 × 2 = 10
2 × 7 = 14	4 − 2 = 2	8 × 4 = 32
7 + 7 = 14	7 × 6 = 42	4 + 0 = 4
3 − 1 = 2	15 − 7 = 8	11 − 2 = 9
8 × 8 = 64	8 + 8 = 16	1 × 4 = 4
11 − 5 = 6	3 × 2 = 6	6 − 4 = 2
6 × 0 = 0	2 + 4 = 6	1 + 4 = 5
9 + 8 = 17	5 + 9 = 14	8 + 9 = 17
1 × 2 = 2	9 × 3 = 27	2 × 8 = 16
2 + 6 = 8	12 − 8 = 4	11 − 3 = 8
10 − 3 = 7	8 × 6 = 48	3 + 2 = 5
5 + 3 = 8	3 + 8 = 11	8 − 7 = 1
12 − 7 = 5	10 − 3 = 7	9 × 2 = 18
	7 × 1 = 7	4 + 7 = 11

Day 23 — Time Required — End Time

2 + 7 = 9	15 − 9 = 6	6 × 6 = 36
7 + 8 = 15	5 × 9 = 45	12 − 9 = 3
6 × 3 = 18	9 + 7 = 16	6 − 4 = 2
5 − 1 = 4	3 + 3 = 6	9 + 2 = 11
7 + 4 = 11	6 × 1 = 6	2 × 9 = 18
4 × 9 = 36	9 + 1 = 10	5 + 2 = 7
9 + 6 = 15	10 − 2 = 8	9 − 6 = 3
11 − 7 = 4	7 − 5 = 2	5 × 4 = 20
2 + 3 = 5	8 + 2 = 10	12 − 4 = 8
7 × 8 = 56	7 × 3 = 21	6 × 2 = 12
3 × 1 = 3	10 − 5 = 5	9 + 4 = 13
10 − 6 = 4	9 × 9 = 81	8 − 4 = 4
8 + 4 = 12	3 × 4 = 12	4 + 2 = 6
5 + 1 = 6	3 + 7 = 10	5 + 7 = 12
5 × 0 = 0	11 − 6 = 5	16 − 8 = 8
11 − 9 = 2	8 × 9 = 72	12 − 7 = 5
1 − 1 = 0	16 − 7 = 9	

Day 24 — Date M D — Start Time

14 − 7 = 7	5 + 8 = 13	9 × 0 = 0
3 + 9 = 12	2 × 8 = 16	6 + 8 = 14
8 − 3 = 5	9 + 0 = 9	1 + 5 = 6
5 × 3 = 15	16 − 8 = 8	3 × 7 = 21
10 − 7 = 3	8 + 5 = 13	5 + 7 = 12
7 + 1 = 8	5 × 6 = 30	9 × 3 = 27
9 + 2 = 11	5 − 4 = 1	7 − 7 = 0
9 − 4 = 5	12 − 3 = 9	14 − 9 = 5
8 × 3 = 24	1 + 3 = 4	9 × 6 = 54
12 − 8 = 4	10 − 1 = 9	11 − 8 = 3
1 × 3 = 3	9 × 8 = 72	7 + 3 = 10
4 + 9 = 13	3 × 3 = 9	8 × 9 = 72
8 − 7 = 1	6 − 4 = 2	5 × 4 = 20
8 + 1 = 9	14 − 6 = 8	2 + 2 = 4
15 − 6 = 9	5 × 5 = 25	4 × 9 = 36
3 × 2 = 6	6 + 4 = 10	7 + 8 = 15
		7 − 3 = 4

Day 24 — Time Required — End Time

7 × 2 = 14	12 − 7 = 5	9 − 6 = 3
8 + 6 = 14	2 × 7 = 14	3 + 6 = 9
14 − 5 = 9	5 + 6 = 11	2 × 4 = 8
8 × 2 = 16	2 × 3 = 6	12 − 9 = 3
11 − 6 = 5	12 − 4 = 8	8 × 4 = 32
1 + 9 = 10	9 − 1 = 8	1 + 1 = 2
3 + 5 = 8	6 + 5 = 11	3 × 1 = 3
6 − 3 = 3	9 × 7 = 63	4 + 8 = 12
7 × 3 = 21	13 − 4 = 9	16 − 7 = 9
9 + 4 = 13	8 × 8 = 64	2 × 5 = 10
8 − 6 = 2	4 + 5 = 9	1 + 6 = 7
3 × 4 = 12	7 + 7 = 14	8 + 3 = 11
0 + 2 = 2	6 × 8 = 48	15 − 8 = 7
8 + 7 = 15	11 − 9 = 2	6 × 3 = 18
5 − 5 = 0	4 + 6 = 10	17 − 9 = 8
1 × 2 = 2	5 + 7 = 12	4 × 3 = 12

79

Day 29 (page 79)

Start Time

6×5=45	9×7=63	5+7=12
6+2=8	9+2=11	11−5=6
13−7=6	4+3=7	9+7=16
9+1=10	2×6=12	3−1=2
7×4=28	7+9=16	2×9=18
9−6=3	6×1=6	10−2=8
11−8=3	8−6=2	1+2=3
4+2=6	11−3=8	3+7=10
10−1=9	8×5=40	7−6=1
2×4=8	15−6=9	3×4=12
2×3=6	7+3=10	14−6=8
5−0=5	6×8=48	9×8=72
11−4=7	2+9=11	6+6=12
7×3=21	5+0=5	7−3=4
2+6=8	9×4=36	3+6=9
7+7=14	3+9=12	13−8=5
	9−8=1	5×5=25

Date: M D

Day 29 (page 80)

12−3=9	8−3=5	6×6=36
5×1=5	1+5=6	9+6=15
9+8=17	5×3=15	10−4=6
8−1=7	10−3=7	9×2=18
4×6=24	9×1=9	15−8=7
16−9=7	1+2=3	7+8=15
6−5=1	5×4=20	3+4=7
6+4=10	2+8=10	8−6=2
5×8=40	13−4=9	6×9=54
14−7=7	3×8=24	4+7=11
5+8=13	8+6=14	3−3=0
8+7=15	14−5=9	7×8=56
6×2=12	3×6=18	0+8=8
11−9=2	11−7=4	10−6=4
7+5=12	7×9=63	9+4=13
6×3=18	6+7=13	7−2=5

Time Required **End Time**

Day 30 (page 81)

Start Time

1+4=5	5+6=11	13−5=8
9×3=27	6−3=3	9×7=63
11−3=8	6+2=8	8+5=13
5+9=14	6+7=13	7×8=56
1−1=0	5×5=25	1×6=6
9×1=9	7−3=4	3+9=12
3+1=4	7×6=42	8−1=7
15−7=8	14−5=9	4×2=8
7×7=49	4+8=12	11−5=6
12−5=7	8×3=24	3+6=9
8+2=10	1+8=9	5+9=14
8−4=4	14−6=8	14−9=5
9+5=14	9−9=0	5×7=35
5+0=5	8×8=64	7−6=1
8×6=48	8+7=15	8×7=56
16−8=8	17−9=8	4×7=28
	3×7=21	2+4=6

Date: M D

Day 30 (page 82)

18−9=9	8+6=14	2×4=8
6+5=11	13−4=9	4+1=5
2×9=18	0×7=0	12−4=8
14−8=6	8−2=6	7+9=16
3×6=18	3×9=27	5×1=5
3+7=10	6+6=12	5×3=15
9−5=4	10−2=8	3+5=8
1+6=7	1+9=10	10−8=2
15−6=9	9×8=72	9+4=13
2+7=9	7−2=5	6×7=42
10−3=7	6×6=36	6×8=48
9+8=17	6−0=6	12−3=9
9−3=6	4+7=11	1+7=8
6×5=30	7×5=35	9×9=81
7+8=15	4×4=16	11−7=4
8×5=40	5+3=8	8+8=16
5−4=1	10−7=3	

Time Required **End Time**

Day 31 (page 85)

Start Time

3+3=6	16−7=9	6×7=42
8×6=48	2×9=18	2+4=6
5−4=1	14−5=9	1×4=4
2×5=10	3+8=11	4×9=36
7+9=16	8+9=17	9−6=3
14−6=8	6×8=48	4+5=9
5+2=7	6+2=8	7+5=12
3×2=6	9×7=63	12−3=9
0×3=0	6−3=3	6×2=12
8−5=3	8+8=16	11−2=9
9+2=11	10−9=1	7−2=5
9−3=6	5+7=12	8×8=64
4+8=12	5×6=30	3+1=4
17−9=8	8−6=2	11−3=8
8+2=10	3+4=7	9+6=15
4×5=20	15−6=9	12−7=5
		8×9=72

Date: M D

Day 31 (page 86)

3+5=8	5×1=5	13−6=7
8+6=14	3×6=18	8+1=9
4−2=2	3+7=10	2−1=1
9×8=72	11−4=7	5×5=25
9+1=10	4×0=0	7−7=0
1×4=4	6+3=9	11−8=3
12−5=7	5+8=13	4+8=12
7−5=2	10−5=5	9×9=81
4+9=13	7×3=21	4+4=8
2×7=14	9×2=18	8+6=13
15−8=7	7+1=8	4×7=28
5+1=6	7+6=13	10−1=9
8−6=2	9−5=4	5×7=35
10−3=7	2×3=6	15−9=6
9+8=17	5×3=15	3+9=12
5×4=20	14−9=5	7×2=14
16−9=7	9+4=13	

Time Required **End Time**

Day 32 (page 87)

Start Time

3−3=0	2+6=8	10−2=8
3+1=4	11−5=6	5+3=8
9×7=63	6+7=13	3×3=9
8+2=10	9×9=81	9+4=13
4×7=28	3−1=2	5−4=1
8−7=1	8×7=56	6×9=54
7+4=11	9+0=9	1−0=1
13−7=6	9×3=27	5+4=9
2+3=5	4×3=12	14−7=7
8×6=48	9−3=6	3×6=18
17−9=8	4+9=13	7+6=13
7+7=14	2×8=16	12−3=9
5×7=35	14−8=6	16−9=7
7−1=6	3×4=12	2×7=14
11−8=3	14−6=8	6+8=14
1×6=6	2×6=12	13−6=7
	9+8=17	7+3=10

Date: M D

Day 32 (page 88)

3×2=6	3+2=5	4×9=36
7−4=3	8×3=24	4−3=1
4+1=5	9−5=4	12−4=8
15−8=7	8+8=16	5+2=7
8+9=17	5×3=15	2+8=10
8×5=40	4+0=4	3×7=21
8×4=32	6×2=12	5−5=0
8+1=9	9+9=18	7+1=8
6×4=24	5−1=4	5×9=45
8−8=0	1×8=8	9+6=15
6×0=0	16−8=8	10−5=5
3+7=10	3+9=12	4+7=11
10−8=2	4×4=16	10−6=4
7×9=63	11−4=7	9×2=18
16−7=9	9+1=10	8+6=14
7+8=15	2×3=6	11−9=2
11−7=4		

Time Required **End Time**

Day 33 — Start Time (89)

4 + 0 = 4	9 × 2 = 18	2 + 5 = 7
7 − 4 = 3	14 − 7 = 7	6 × 3 = 18
5 × 3 = 15	2 + 7 = 9	8 − 1 = 7
10 − 4 = 6	7 × 9 = 63	6 + 8 = 14
5 + 2 = 7	13 − 8 = 5	6 × 7 = 42
3 × 4 = 12	5 × 1 = 5	1 + 8 = 9
8 − 7 = 1	7 + 4 = 11	8 × 6 = 48
5 × 5 = 25	9 − 4 = 5	5 + 3 = 8
17 − 9 = 8	3 + 2 = 5	10 − 6 = 4
0 × 7 = 0	8 − 3 = 5	4 − 0 = 4
8 + 8 = 16	7 × 4 = 28	7 + 5 = 12
4 × 2 = 8	6 + 7 = 13	8 × 8 = 64
2 × 9 = 18	7 − 3 = 4	10 − 1 = 9
9 + 7 = 16	9 + 3 = 11	10 − 8 = 2
15 − 6 = 9	7 × 7 = 49	2 × 2 = 4
8 + 3 = 11	2 + 9 = 11	13 − 7 = 6
	12 − 3 = 9	9 + 2 = 11

Day 33 — End Time

9 − 3 = 6	0 + 6 = 6	9 × 4 = 36
16 − 7 = 9	8 − 4 = 4	2 − 1 = 1
3 + 5 = 8	3 × 9 = 27	6 + 3 = 9
8 × 1 = 8	6 × 4 = 24	11 − 2 = 9
14 − 9 = 5	3 + 9 = 12	9 × 8 = 72
2 × 8 = 16	5 × 8 = 40	5 + 5 = 10
7 + 2 = 9	11 − 9 = 2	6 × 6 = 36
11 − 6 = 5	7 + 1 = 8	5 + 9 = 14
4 − 4 = 0	4 × 8 = 32	8 × 2 = 16
5 × 7 = 35	7 + 9 = 16	4 + 9 = 13
11 − 4 = 7	9 − 1 = 8	9 − 7 = 2
8 + 6 = 14	8 × 4 = 32	12 − 8 = 4
7 × 6 = 42	12 − 7 = 5	3 + 8 = 11
9 + 9 = 18	3 + 3 = 6	2 × 5 = 10
18 − 9 = 9	13 − 9 = 4	5 + 8 = 13
2 + 8 = 10	3 × 3 = 9	10 − 2 = 8
0 × 9 = 0	4 + 7 = 11	

Day 34 — Start Time (91)

2 × 5 = 10	8 × 2 = 16	8 − 5 = 3
9 − 1 = 8	6 − 5 = 1	4 + 1 = 5
4 + 2 = 6	1 + 0 = 1	1 × 9 = 9
3 × 2 = 6	5 − 3 = 2	11 − 6 = 5
2 + 9 = 11	7 × 7 = 49	9 + 3 = 12
7 − 4 = 3	15 − 7 = 8	5 × 8 = 40
12 − 3 = 9	3 + 4 = 7	4 − 1 = 3
7 × 8 = 56	8 + 9 = 17	9 × 8 = 72
10 − 4 = 6	9 − 8 = 1	8 + 1 = 9
8 + 4 = 12	3 × 1 = 3	14 − 7 = 7
5 + 5 = 10	13 − 6 = 7	7 + 7 = 14
9 × 6 = 54	6 × 6 = 36	9 × 2 = 18
3 + 3 = 6	3 + 7 = 10	5 − 3 = 8
5 × 6 = 30	10 − 9 = 1	12 − 6 = 6
0 × 7 = 0	9 + 5 = 14	3 × 3 = 9
8 + 5 = 13	15 − 9 = 6	5 + 7 = 12
	4 × 3 = 12	10 − 6 = 4

Day 34 — End Time

5 × 6 = 30	3 + 5 = 8	3 − 1 = 2
8 − 1 = 7	9 + 8 = 17	1 × 5 = 5
6 + 8 = 14	7 × 4 = 28	6 + 7 = 13
11 − 9 = 2	4 − 3 = 1	4 + 0 = 4
8 × 4 = 32	8 + 8 = 16	8 × 9 = 72
2 + 2 = 4	2 × 9 = 18	4 + 6 = 10
9 − 4 = 5	5 + 6 = 11	8 − 3 = 5
7 × 1 = 7	14 − 8 = 6	1 + 1 = 2
13 − 8 = 5	7 + 1 = 8	6 × 8 = 48
4 × 7 = 28	11 − 3 = 8	10 − 7 = 3
6 − 2 = 4	8 × 8 = 64	3 × 8 = 24
2 + 4 = 6	11 − 7 = 4	2 + 8 = 10
8 + 6 = 14	5 × 9 = 45	6 × 7 = 42
11 − 4 = 7	9 + 9 = 18	12 − 5 = 7
9 × 9 = 81	4 + 9 = 13	4 × 8 = 32
15 − 6 = 9	10 − 2 = 8	
	4 × 9 = 36	

Day 35 — Start Time (93)

10 − 6 = 4	2 × 5 = 10	13 − 7 = 6
5 + 0 = 5	9 + 9 = 18	9 − 9 = 0
7 × 7 = 49	5 − 3 = 2	6 + 1 = 7
8 − 7 = 1	18 − 9 = 9	3 + 7 = 10
4 + 4 = 8	7 + 2 = 9	6 − 3 = 3
13 − 5 = 8	5 × 9 = 45	8 × 5 = 40
7 × 3 = 21	7 + 6 = 13	15 − 8 = 7
3 × 8 = 24	9 − 7 = 2	4 + 6 = 10
5 + 4 = 9	4 × 6 = 24	8 × 9 = 72
9 + 5 = 14	11 − 2 = 9	3 + 4 = 7
5 × 7 = 35	4 × 9 = 36	2 × 3 = 6
13 − 9 = 4	2 + 8 = 10	10 − 9 = 1
3 + 8 = 11	7 × 0 = 0	7 × 6 = 42
9 − 2 = 7	2 + 5 = 7	7 + 7 = 14
9 × 8 = 72	10 − 5 = 5	9 × 7 = 63
4 + 7 = 11	8 + 7 = 15	13 − 8 = 5
	6 × 5 = 30	

Day 35 — End Time

8 − 4 = 4	6 × 7 = 42	16 − 8 = 8
0 + 3 = 3	7 + 3 = 10	5 × 5 = 25
7 × 4 = 28	14 − 5 = 9	9 + 1 = 10
15 − 6 = 9	6 × 9 = 54	2 + 3 = 5
4 × 4 = 16	14 − 7 = 7	9 × 2 = 18
9 − 4 = 5	8 + 4 = 12	4 − 4 = 0
8 × 7 = 56	2 + 6 = 8	6 + 2 = 8
6 + 6 = 12	9 − 5 = 4	3 − 1 = 2
14 − 9 = 5	2 × 4 = 8	4 × 2 = 8
9 × 6 = 54	4 + 8 = 12	17 − 9 = 8
1 + 7 = 8	4 − 3 = 1	8 + 9 = 17
7 + 9 = 16	7 × 2 = 14	3 × 5 = 15
11 − 5 = 6	5 + 3 = 8	5 + 8 = 13
5 × 2 = 10	15 − 7 = 8	7 × 8 = 56
12 − 9 = 3	8 + 6 = 14	10 − 1 = 9
2 × 2 = 4	12 − 9 = 3	7 + 4 = 11
7 + 5 = 12	8 × 1 = 8	

Day 36 — Start Time (97)

4 × 9 = 36	8 × 2 = 16	13 − 5 = 8
13 − 4 = 9	4 + 0 = 4	1 + 7 = 8
7 + 8 = 15	6 × 4 = 24	2 × 3 = 6
6 + 6 = 12	1 × 3 = 3	9 − 4 = 5
5 × 9 = 45	8 − 6 = 2	4 × 2 = 8
3 + 2 = 5	5 + 3 = 8	6 + 5 = 11
1 × 5 = 5	5 + 9 = 14	12 − 4 = 8
7 − 2 = 5	14 − 6 = 8	4 + 1 = 5
8 + 8 = 16	5 × 5 = 25	3 × 4 = 12
16 − 7 = 9	10 − 6 = 6	5 × 3 = 15
9 + 3 = 12	7 − 3 = 4	6 − 2 = 4
4 × 3 = 12	7 × 6 = 42	4 + 6 = 10
9 − 5 = 4	1 + 5 = 6	5 − 2 = 3
2 + 7 = 9	13 − 8 = 5	8 + 5 = 13
9 × 3 = 27	7 + 6 = 13	11 − 2 = 9
10 − 9 = 1	12 − 8 = 4	4 + 9 = 13
	9 × 8 = 72	6 × 8 = 48

Day 36 — End Time (98)

9 × 2 = 18	15 − 6 = 9	4 + 2 = 6
7 × 5 = 35	8 + 1 = 9	8 + 9 = 17
9 + 2 = 11	2 − 2 = 0	5 − 4 = 1
17 − 9 = 8	3 × 2 = 6	7 × 8 = 56
8 × 0 = 0	6 − 2 = 4	6 + 7 = 13
4 + 3 = 7	10 − 1 = 9	9 × 6 = 54
5 + 8 = 13	9 + 6 = 15	15 − 7 = 8
12 − 5 = 7	5 × 6 = 30	9 − 8 = 1
9 × 5 = 45	5 + 1 = 6	9 + 9 = 18
2 × 7 = 14	8 + 6 = 14	6 × 7 = 42
1 + 8 = 9	6 × 3 = 18	10 − 2 = 8
3 + 7 = 10	13 − 6 = 7	4 − 3 = 1
8 − 5 = 3	3 × 7 = 21	16 − 9 = 7
3 × 3 = 9	14 − 9 = 5	6 + 8 = 14
3 × 9 = 27	1 + 9 = 10	4 × 8 = 32
12 − 7 = 5	7 × 1 = 7	
6 + 4 = 10	18 − 9 = 9	

117

118

121

122

123

124

125

126

169

Day 53

Start Time · **End Time**

12 − 6 = 6	2 + 7 = 9	9 × 8 = 72
6 + 2 = 8	4 − 0 = 4	1 + 6 = 7
3 − 2 = 1	6 × 7 = 42	6 + 7 = 13
13 − 8 = 5	9 + 7 = 16	3 × 8 = 24
4 × 3 = 12	8 × 0 = 0	9 × 7 = 63
9 + 6 = 15	1 + 3 = 4	9 − 1 = 8
3 × 3 = 9	7 × 9 = 63	6 + 3 = 9
8 + 1 = 9	3 + 5 = 8	6 − 2 = 4
4 − 3 = 1	5 + 8 = 13	10 − 1 = 9
4 + 8 = 12	9 − 4 = 5	8 + 3 = 11
5 × 1 = 5	3 + 7 = 10	3 × 7 = 21
9 − 3 = 6	12 − 3 = 9	11 − 9 = 2
7 + 8 = 15	3 × 2 = 6	9 × 6 = 54
6 + 5 = 11	10 − 6 = 4	2 × 6 = 12
7 × 3 = 21	8 × 7 = 56	7 + 3 = 10
17 − 9 = 8	12 − 4 = 8	18 − 9 = 9
	2 + 8 = 10	4 × 7 = 28

Day 53

Time Required · **End Time**

5 + 1 = 6	2 × 7 = 14	2 − 1 = 1
7 − 7 = 0	7 + 2 = 9	10 − 9 = 1
9 + 1 = 10	6 − 1 = 5	5 + 4 = 9
6 × 5 = 30	17 − 8 = 9	3 × 6 = 18
8 + 7 = 15	8 × 1 = 8	11 − 3 = 8
9 × 3 = 27	11 − 4 = 7	6 × 8 = 48
10 − 5 = 5	1 + 9 = 10	3 + 3 = 6
0 + 6 = 6	3 + 8 = 11	15 − 6 = 9
5 × 7 = 35	9 × 5 = 45	7 − 5 = 2
4 + 6 = 10	7 + 4 = 11	2 × 8 = 16
7 − 4 = 3	9 − 8 = 1	9 + 9 = 18
2 × 2 = 4	2 × 4 = 8	13 − 9 = 4
15 − 8 = 7	7 + 9 = 16	4 × 6 = 24
4 + 3 = 7	4 × 6 = 24	8 × 6 = 48
11 − 7 = 4	9 + 2 = 11	10 − 7 = 3
14 − 9 = 5	14 − 9 = 5	6 + 9 = 15
8 + 4 = 12	7 × 4 = 28	

Day 54

Start Time · **End Time** · Date · M · D

8 − 3 = 5	4 − 3 = 1	3 + 3 = 6
9 × 4 = 36	4 × 8 = 32	9 × 2 = 18
3 − 2 = 1	2 + 7 = 9	4 − 4 = 0
6 + 9 = 15	17 − 9 = 8	7 × 5 = 35
12 − 4 = 8	3 + 7 = 10	4 + 2 = 6
2 + 1 = 3	1 × 9 = 9	1 + 9 = 10
3 × 2 = 6	8 − 7 = 1	5 − 1 = 4
6 − 4 = 2	2 × 4 = 8	6 + 2 = 8
5 × 2 = 10	3 + 6 = 9	8 × 4 = 32
13 − 9 = 4	10 − 3 = 7	5 × 6 = 30
8 × 5 = 40	8 + 4 = 12	7 + 9 = 16
7 + 2 = 9	4 + 3 = 7	4 + 8 = 12
14 − 7 = 7	9 × 5 = 45	10 − 5 = 5
8 + 7 = 15	14 − 9 = 5	9 × 7 = 63
13 − 5 = 8	4 × 4 = 16	11 − 8 = 3
6 × 5 = 30	11 − 7 = 4	3 × 5 = 15
		8 + 6 = 14

Day 54

Time Required · **End Time**

2 + 2 = 4	6 − 1 = 5	5 × 9 = 45
6 + 8 = 14	5 + 4 = 9	4 + 8 = 12
7 × 2 = 14	9 + 3 = 12	15 − 7 = 8
9 − 4 = 5	2 + 5 = 7	5 − 3 = 2
1 + 7 = 8	9 × 6 = 54	4 × 6 = 24
8 + 1 = 9	10 − 8 = 2	7 − 0 = 7
6 × 3 = 18	6 + 4 = 10	5 + 3 = 8
11 − 8 = 3	9 − 5 = 4	6 × 8 = 48
4 + 6 = 10	3 + 4 = 7	13 − 8 = 5
16 − 9 = 7	2 × 2 = 4	9 × 3 = 27
3 × 7 = 21	13 − 6 = 7	9 + 5 = 14
9 + 4 = 13	2 × 5 = 10	8 − 6 = 2
8 × 2 = 16	8 + 5 = 13	5 × 3 = 15
15 − 6 = 9	7 × 6 = 42	6 + 6 = 12
7 + 4 = 11	14 − 5 = 9	10 − 4 = 6
12 − 8 = 4	5 × 8 = 40	4 × 5 = 20
2 × 9 = 18	17 − 8 = 9	

Day 55

Start Time · **End Time** · Date · M · D

1 + 3 = 4	16 − 8 = 8	3 × 9 = 27
6 − 5 = 1	4 − 1 = 3	4 + 2 = 6
5 + 7 = 12	7 + 2 = 9	7 + 9 = 16
11 − 8 = 3	5 + 6 = 11	8 × 5 = 40
3 × 7 = 21	8 − 7 = 1	9 − 1 = 8
9 + 8 = 17	4 × 9 = 36	12 − 8 = 4
6 × 9 = 54	6 × 2 = 12	4 + 5 = 9
9 − 5 = 4	7 − 2 = 5	8 − 3 = 5
15 − 7 = 8	3 × 6 = 18	9 × 8 = 72
3 × 3 = 9	6 + 0 = 6	1 + 2 = 3
3 + 9 = 12	9 + 9 = 18	0 × 7 = 0
8 × 6 = 48	6 × 5 = 30	9 + 3 = 12
5 + 3 = 8	16 − 7 = 9	11 − 2 = 9
7 × 8 = 56	7 × 3 = 21	8 × 3 = 24
9 + 4 = 13	2 + 8 = 10	14 − 6 = 8
10 − 6 = 4	11 − 5 = 6	9 × 7 = 63
	2 × 3 = 6	5 + 8 = 13

Day 55

Time Required · **End Time**

9 + 6 = 15	10 − 1 = 9	8 − 0 = 8
4 × 5 = 20	3 + 7 = 10	3 + 6 = 9
11 − 9 = 2	9 × 2 = 18	4 × 2 = 8
5 × 8 = 40	5 + 4 = 9	9 × 4 = 36
5 + 5 = 10	3 × 8 = 24	6 − 2 = 4
12 − 3 = 9	7 − 3 = 4	14 − 8 = 6
6 + 2 = 8	1 + 6 = 7	7 × 4 = 28
7 − 1 = 6	14 − 7 = 7	5 + 8 = 13
8 × 8 = 64	6 − 4 = 2	11 − 4 = 7
4 + 7 = 11	7 × 7 = 49	4 × 6 = 24
4 − 2 = 2	9 + 1 = 10	3 + 1 = 4
2 × 5 = 10	3 × 4 = 12	8 + 7 = 15
5 + 1 = 6	8 + 9 = 17	13 − 5 = 8
4 × 3 = 12	12 − 7 = 5	6 × 6 = 36
5 × 6 = 30	4 + 6 = 10	11 − 9 = 2
2 + 9 = 11	5 × 3 = 15	9 × 3 = 27
12 − 5 = 7	6 + 6 = 12	

Day 56

Start Time · **End Time** · Date · M · D

8 − 7 = 1	7 × 2 = 14	11 − 9 = 2
7 + 9 = 16	3 + 5 = 8	3 × 6 = 18
3 + 3 = 6	14 − 7 = 7	15 − 8 = 7
3 × 7 = 21	7 − 1 = 6	2 + 8 = 10
5 + 5 = 10	4 + 6 = 10	9 − 2 = 7
10 − 6 = 4	10 − 8 = 2	8 + 5 = 13
1 + 8 = 9	5 × 6 = 30	3 + 4 = 7
7 × 6 = 42	6 + 1 = 7	2 × 7 = 14
11 − 5 = 6	5 × 8 = 40	5 − 4 = 1
5 × 2 = 10	8 − 2 = 6	9 × 8 = 72
3 − 1 = 2	7 × 1 = 7	10 − 3 = 7
0 + 2 = 2	9 + 2 = 11	8 + 2 = 10
12 − 8 = 4	5 + 7 = 12	6 × 5 = 30
6 × 3 = 18	3 × 4 = 12	14 − 6 = 8
2 + 9 = 11	13 − 5 = 8	3 + 1 = 4
4 × 4 = 16	6 × 9 = 54	5 × 4 = 20
		6 + 6 = 12

Day 56

Time Required · **End Time**

6 + 2 = 8	5 − 1 = 4	8 × 5 = 40
8 − 4 = 4	7 + 8 = 15	11 − 2 = 9
3 × 5 = 15	3 + 2 = 5	5 + 9 = 14
10 − 4 = 6	4 × 7 = 28	14 − 8 = 6
9 + 6 = 15	5 + 6 = 11	6 − 2 = 4
8 × 8 = 64	9 × 6 = 54	3 + 3 = 6
1 − 1 = 0	12 − 7 = 5	6 × 2 = 12
2 × 2 = 4	8 − 3 = 5	16 − 7 = 9
4 + 2 = 6	7 + 6 = 13	3 + 7 = 10
8 + 6 = 14	4 × 5 = 20	9 × 5 = 45
7 × 3 = 21	6 − 4 = 2	1 + 5 = 6
13 − 8 = 5	2 + 7 = 9	9 + 4 = 13
8 × 7 = 56	5 × 9 = 45	9 − 3 = 6
11 − 3 = 8	11 − 6 = 5	12 − 4 = 8
4 + 7 = 11	7 × 5 = 35	13 − 6 = 7
8 × 2 = 16	16 − 9 = 7	18 − 9 = 9
3 × 9 = 27		

Pre-training Prefrontal Cortex Evaluation········ ☐ M ☐ D

Please evaluate your brain function before beginning the training.

I. Counting Test

Measure the time required for you to count from 1 to 120 aloud as fast as you can.

☐ sec.

II. Word Memorization Test

Memorize as many words as you can **within two minutes.**

account	noon	section	tube	corner	fruit
bear	folder	pottery	extract	thought	music
dew	office	point	store	wheel	life
brother	paper	rest	syrup	color	belt
mind	thunder	hole	problem	magic	safe

Write out as many words as you can remember **in two minutes** on the back of this page. How many words can you remember?

Number of words memorized ☐ words

Word Memorization Test Answers

Stroop Test (Pre-training)

This test should be taken only once. Before you take the test, please get used to the procedure by using the practice chart below. Name the colors the words are printed in aloud as fast as you can. If you make a mistake, name the color again correctly.

(**Example : Red** should be "**blue**." **Red** should be "**green**." **Red** should be "**red**.")

[Practice Chart]

Green	Red	Yellow	Green	Blue

Were you able to name the colors correctly (Blue, yellow, red, green and then yellow)?

Now let's proceed to the test. Fill in the "Start Time" box below and start naming the colors of the words printed on the chart. After you finish the test, fill in the "End Time" box and calculate the time required.

Start Time ☐ : ☐

Red	Blue	Red	Yellow	Green
Green	Red	Green	Yellow	Blue
Green	Blue	Green	Yellow	Red
Blue	Yellow	Yellow	Blue	Green
Red	Blue	Red	Yellow	Green
Green	Yellow	Blue	Red	Red
Green	Yellow	Red	Green	Blue
Blue	Green	Yellow	Red	Blue
Red	Green	Yellow	Yellow	Blue
Blue	Blue	Red	Yellow	Green

End Time ☐ : ☐   **Time Required** ☐ : ☐

Stroop Test (Week 1)

This test should be taken only once. Before you take the test, please get used to the procedure by using the practice chart below. Name the colors the words are printed in aloud as fast as you can. If you make a mistake, name the color again correctly.

(**Example :** Red should be "**blue**." Red should be "**green**." **Red** should be "**red**.")

[Practice Chart]

Green	Red	Yellow	Green	Blue

Were you able to name the colors correctly (Blue, yellow, red, green and then yellow)?

Now let's proceed to the test. Fill in the "Start Time" box below and start naming the colors of the words printed on the chart. After you finish the test, fill in the "End Time" box and calculate the time required.

Start Time [ ] : [ ]

Red	Green	Green	Yellow	Blue
Red	Blue	Red	Yellow	Green
Yellow	Red	Red	Green	Blue
Yellow	Blue	Green	Red	Blue
Red	Blue	Red	Yellow	Green
Green	Yellow	Red	Green	Blue
Blue	Blue	Yellow	Yellow	Green
Green	Yellow	Red	Green	Blue
Red	Yellow	Blue	Green	Yellow
Blue	Red	Yellow	Blue	Green

End Time [ ] : [ ]   Time Required [ ] : [ ]

Stroop Test (Week 2)

This test should be taken only once. Before you take the test, please get used to the procedure by using the practice chart below. Name the colors the words are printed in aloud as fast as you can. If you make a mistake, name the color again correctly.

(**Example : Red** should be "**blue**." **Red** should be "**green**." **Red** should be "**red**.")

[Practice Chart]

Green	Red	Yellow	Green	Blue

Were you able to name the colors correctly (Blue, yellow, red, green and then yellow)?

Now let's proceed to the test. Fill in the "Start Time" box below and start naming the colors of the words printed on the chart. After you finish the test, fill in the "End Time" box and calculate the time required.

Start Time ☐ : ☐

Green	Yellow	Red	Green	Blue
Yellow	Green	Green	Blue	Red
Red	Red	Yellow	Green	Blue
Blue	Green	Yellow	Blue	Red
Yellow	Green	Red	Blue	Red
Red	Green	Green	Yellow	Blue
Yellow	Blue	Blue	Yellow	Green
Red	Blue	Green	Red	Yellow
Green	Yellow	Blue	Yellow	Red
Blue	Blue	Red	Yellow	Green

End Time ☐ : ☐   **Time Required** ☐ : ☐

Stroop Test (Week 3)

This test should be taken only once. Before you take the test, please get used to the procedure by using the practice chart below. Name the colors the words are printed in aloud as fast as you can. If you make a mistake, name the color again correctly.

(**Example :** Red should be "**blue**." Red should be "**green**." **Red** should be "**red**.")

[Practice Chart]

Green	Red	**Yellow**	Green	Blue

Were you able to name the colors correctly (Blue, yellow, red, green and then yellow)?

Now let's proceed to the test. Fill in the "Start Time" box below and start naming the colors of the words printed on the chart. After you finish the test, fill in the "End Time" box and calculate the time required.

Start Time ☐ : ☐

Blue	Green	Red	Yellow	**Green**
Yellow	**Blue**	Green	Yellow	Red
Green	**Yellow**	**Blue**	Blue	Red
Yellow	Blue	Green	Red	**Blue**
Yellow	Yellow	Blue	Blue	Green
Blue	Green	**Red**	Red	Yellow
Blue	**Green**	**Yellow**	Green	Red
Red	Blue	Red	**Yellow**	Green
Green	Green	Yellow	**Red**	Blue
Red	Yellow	Red	Blue	**Green**

End Time ☐ : ☐   Time Required ☐ : ☐

Stroop Test (Week 4)

This test should be taken only once. Before you take the test, please get used to the procedure by using the practice chart below. Name the colors the words are printed in aloud as fast as you can. If you make a mistake, name the color again correctly.

(**Example :** Red should be "blue." Red should be "green." **Red** should be "red.")

[Practice Chart]

Green	**Red**	**Yellow**	Green	**Blue**

Were you able to name the colors correctly (Blue, yellow, red, green and then yellow)?

Now let's proceed to the test. Fill in the "Start Time" box below and start naming the colors of the words printed on the chart. After you finish the test, fill in the "End Time" box and calculate the time required.

Start Time [ ] : [ ]

Red	Yellow	**Blue**	Green	**Red**
Blue	Red	Green	**Yellow**	Blue
Red	**Blue**	Yellow	Blue	Green
Blue	**Yellow**	Green	Red	Red
Red	Blue	Green	Green	Yellow
Green	Red	**Green**	Blue	**Yellow**
Yellow	Red	Yellow	**Blue**	Green
Green	**Green**	Yellow	**Blue**	Red
Blue	**Green**	Red	Yellow	Red
Yellow	Yellow	**Blue**	Blue	Green

End Time [ ] : [ ]   **Time Required** [ ] : [ ]

Stroop Test (Week 5)

This test should be taken only once. Before you take the test, please get used to the procedure by using the practice chart below. Name the colors the words are printed in aloud as fast as you can. If you make a mistake, name the color again correctly.

(**Example :** Red should be "**blue**." Red should be "**green**." **Red** should be "**red**.")

[Practice Chart]

Green	Red	Yellow	Green	Blue

Were you able to name the colors correctly (Blue, yellow, red, green and then yellow)?

Now let's proceed to the test. Fill in the "Start Time" box below and start naming the colors of the words printed on the chart. After you finish the test, fill in the "End Time" box and calculate the time required.

Start Time ☐ : ☐

Red	Blue	Red	Yellow	Green
Green	Yellow	Red	Green	Blue
Blue	Blue	Yellow	Yellow	Green
Yellow	Blue	Green	Blue	Red
Green	Yellow	Red	Green	Blue
Green	Green	Red	Yellow	Blue
Red	Red	Yellow	Blue	Green
Red	Red	Green	Yellow	Blue
Red	Green	Yellow	Yellow	Blue
Blue	Red	Yellow	Blue	Green

End Time ☐ : ☐　　**Time Required** ☐ : ☐

Stroop Test (Week 6)

This test should be taken only once. Before you take the test, please get used to the procedure by using the practice chart below. Name the colors the words are printed in aloud as fast as you can. If you make a mistake, name the color again correctly.

(**Example :** Red should be "**blue**." Red should be "**green**." Red should be "**red**.")

[Practice Chart]

Green	Red	**Yellow**	Green	Blue

Were you able to name the colors correctly (Blue, yellow, red, green and then yellow)?

Now let's proceed to the test. Fill in the "Start Time" box below and start naming the colors of the words printed on the chart. After you finish the test, fill in the "End Time" box and calculate the time required.

Start Time [   ] : [   ]

Yellow	**Green**	Red	Green	Blue
Red	Yellow	**Blue**	**Red**	Green
Red	**Red**	Blue	Green	**Yellow**
Red	Green	Yellow	Yellow	**Blue**
Red	**Blue**	Red	Yellow	Green
Green	Yellow	Red	Green	**Blue**
Blue	Blue	**Yellow**	Yellow	Blue
Yellow	**Blue**	Green	Red	Blue
Green	Yellow	Red	**Green**	Blue
Blue	Yellow	**Red**	Blue	Green

End Time [   ] : [   ]   **Time Required** [   ] : [   ]

Stroop Test (Week 7)

This test should be taken only once. Before you take the test, please get used to the procedure by using the practice chart below. Name the colors the words are printed in aloud as fast as you can. If you make a mistake, name the color again correctly.

(**Example :** Red should be "**blue**." Red should be "**green**." **Red** should be "**red**.")

[Practice Chart]

Green   Red   **Yellow**   Green   Blue

Were you able to name the colors correctly (Blue, yellow, red, green and then yellow)?

Now let's proceed to the test. Fill in the "Start Time" box below and start naming the colors of the words printed on the chart. After you finish the test, fill in the "End Time" box and calculate the time required.

Start Time [ ] : [ ]

Green	Red	Green	**Yellow**	Blue
Yellow	Green	**Blue**	Yellow	Red
Red	Yellow	**Blue**	Red	Green
Yellow	**Green**	Red	Green	Blue
Blue	**Red**	Yellow	Blue	Green
Red	Blue	Red	Green	**Yellow**
Green	Yellow	Red	**Blue**	Green
Red	**Red**	Green	Blue	Yellow
Blue	Blue	Blue	Yellow	**Yellow**
Blue	Red	Green	Blue	Yellow

End Time [ ] : [ ]   **Time Required** [ ] : [ ]

x

Stroop Test (Week 8)

This test should be taken only once. Before you take the test, please get used to the procedure by using the practice chart below. Name the colors the words are printed in aloud as fast as you can. If you make a mistake, name the color again correctly.

(**Example** : Red should be "**blue**." Red should be "**green**." **Red** should be "**red**.")

[Practice Chart]

Green	Red	**Yellow**	Green	Blue

Were you able to name the colors correctly (Blue, yellow, red, green and then yellow)?

Now let's proceed to the test. Fill in the "Start Time" box below and start naming the colors of the words printed on the chart. After you finish the test, fill in the "End Time" box and calculate the time required.

Start Time ☐ : ☐

Blue	Green	Blue	**Red**	Yellow
Yellow	Green	**Green**	Red	Blue
Green	Yellow	Red	Yellow	**Blue**
Red	Red	Yellow	Green	**Blue**
Yellow	Blue	Blue	Blue	Yellow
Red	Green	Yellow	**Green**	Blue
Green	**Yellow**	Red	Blue	Red
Blue	Green	**Green**	Yellow	Red
Red	**Red**	Green	Yellow	Blue
Blue	Red	**Blue**	Green	Yellow

End Time ☐ : ☐   **Time Required** ☐ : ☐

Stroop Test (Week 9)

This test should be taken only once. Before you take the test, please get used to the procedure by using the practice chart below. Name the colors the words are printed in aloud as fast as you can. If you make a mistake, name the color again correctly.

(**Example** : **Red** should be "**blue**." **Red** should be "**green**." **Red** should be "**red**.")

[Practice Chart]

| Green | Red | Yellow | Green | Blue |

Were you able to name the colors correctly (Blue, yellow, red, green and then yellow)?

Now let's proceed to the test. Fill in the "Start Time" box below and start naming the colors of the words printed on the chart. After you finish the test, fill in the "End Time" box and calculate the time required.

Start Time [ ] : [ ]

Blue	Red	Blue	Green	Yellow
Red	Blue	Green	Yellow	Red
Yellow	Green	Blue	Red	Red
Green	Red	Green	Blue	Yellow
Blue	Yellow	Blue	Blue	Yellow
Blue	Green	Red	Yellow	Blue
Green	Red	Blue	Yellow	Green
Green	Red	Yellow	Blue	Yellow
Yellow	Blue	Red	Green	Red
Blue	Yellow	Red	Green	Green

End Time [ ] : [ ]   **Time Required** [ ] : [ ]

Stroop Test (Week 10)

This test should be taken only once. Before you take the test, please get used to the procedure by using the practice chart below. Name the colors the words are printed in aloud as fast as you can. If you make a mistake, name the color again correctly.

(**Example :** Red should be "**blue**." Red should be "**green**." Red should be "**red**.")

[Practice Chart]

Green	Red	Yellow	Green	Blue

Were you able to name the colors correctly (Blue, yellow, red, green and then yellow)?

Now let's proceed to the test. Fill in the "Start Time" box below and start naming the colors of the words printed on the chart. After you finish the test, fill in the "End Time" box and calculate the time required.

Start Time [   ] : [   ]

Blue	Green	Red	Yellow	Blue
Green	Red	Blue	Yellow	Green
Yellow	Red	Yellow	Green	Blue
Blue	Yellow	Blue	Blue	Yellow
Red	Yellow	Green	Green	Blue
Blue	Green	Yellow	Blue	Red
Red	Red	Blue	Green	Yellow
Yellow	Blue	Green	Red	Red
Green	Blue	Red	Yellow	Red
Red	Green	Green	Yellow	Blue

End Time [   ] : [   ]   **Time Required** [   ] : [   ]

Stroop Test (Week 11)

This test should be taken only once. Before you take the test, please get used to the procedure by using the practice chart below. Name the colors the words are printed in aloud as fast as you can. If you make a mistake, name the color again correctly.

(**Example :** Red should be "**blue**." Red should be "**green**." **Red** should be "**red**.")

[Practice Chart]

Green	**Red**	**Yellow**	Green	**Blue**

Were you able to name the colors correctly (Blue, yellow, red, green and then yellow)?

Now let's proceed to the test. Fill in the "Start Time" box below and start naming the colors of the words printed on the chart. After you finish the test, fill in the "End Time" box and calculate the time required.

Start Time [ ] : [ ]

Yellow	**Blue**	Green	**Red**	Red
Green	**Blue**	Yellow	**Red**	Red
Yellow	Yellow	**Blue**	Blue	**Blue**
Blue	Green	**Red**	**Blue**	Yellow
Yellow	**Blue**	**Green**	**Red**	**Yellow**
Green	**Red**	**Green**	Blue	**Yellow**
Red	**Red**	Blue	**Yellow**	**Green**
Red	**Yellow**	**Green**	Green	**Blue**
Red	Green	**Green**	**Yellow**	**Blue**
Blue	**Green**	Red	**Blue**	**Yellow**

End Time [ ] : [ ]   **Time Required** [ ] : [ ]

Stroop Test (Week 12)

This test should be taken only once. Before you take the test, please get used to the procedure by using the practice chart below. Name the colors the words are printed in aloud as fast as you can. If you make a mistake, name the color again correctly.

(**Example :** Red should be "**blue**." Red should be "**green**." **Red** should be "**red**.")

[Practice Chart]

Green	Red	Yellow	Green	Blue

Were you able to name the colors correctly (Blue, yellow, red, green and then yellow)?

Now let's proceed to the test. Fill in the "Start Time" box below and start naming the colors of the words printed on the chart. After you finish the test, fill in the "End Time" box and calculate the time required.

Start Time [ ] : [ ]

Red	Yellow	Green	Blue	Red
Red	Red	Yellow	Green	Blue
Blue	Yellow	Red	Blue	Green
Green	Green	Red	Blue	Yellow
Yellow	Blue	Green	Red	Yellow
Blue	Yellow	Red	Blue	Green
Green	Blue	Yellow	Red	Red
Yellow	Blue	Blue	Yellow	Blue
Green	Green	Red	Yellow	Blue
Red	Green	Green	Yellow	Blue

End Time [ ] : [ ]   **Time Required** [ ] : [ ]

DR KAWASHIMA

TRAIN YOUR BRAIN

60 Days to a Better Brain

PENGUIN BOOKS

Published by the Penguin Group
Penguin Books Ltd, 80 Strand, London WC2R 0RL, England
Penguin Group (USA) Inc., 375 Hudson Street, New York, New York 10014, USA
Penguin Group (Canada), 90 Eglinton Avenue East, Suite 700, Toronto, Ontario, Canada M4P 2Y3
(a division of Pearson Penguin Canada Inc.)
Penguin Ireland, 25 St Stephen's Green, Dublin 2, Ireland (a division of Penguin Books Ltd)
Penguin Group (Australia), 250 Camberwell Road, Camberwell,
Victoria 3124, Australia (a division of Pearson Australia Group Pty Ltd)
Penguin Books India Pvt Ltd, 11 Community Centre,
Panchsheel Park, New Delhi – 110 017, India
Penguin Group (NZ), 67 Apollo Drive, Mairangi Bay, Auckland 1310, New Zealand
(a division of Pearson New Zealand Ltd)
Penguin Books (South Africa) (Pty) Ltd, 24 Sturdee Avenue,
Rosebank, Johannesburg 2196, South Africa

Penguin Books Ltd, Registered Offices: 80 Strand, London WC2R 0RL, England

www.penguin.com

First published by Kumon 2005
Published by Penguin 2007
1

Copyright © Ryuta Kawashima/Kumon Publishing Co. Ltd, 2005
All rights reserved

Cover and interior design by Shinju Onuki
Illustrations by Yasuko Toyoshima

We are so confident that this will work that, if your brain hasn't improved
in 60 days of doing the exercises, we'll give you your money back. Simply
send back the completed workbook along with your receipt to Dr Kawashima,
Penguin Reference, 80 Strand, London WC2R 0RL. Happy brain training.

The moral right of the author has been asserted

Printed and bound in Italy by Graphicom, srl

ISBN: 978–1–846–14004–4